Praise for Gary Marx's
Twenty-One Trends for the 21ˢᵗ Century:
Out of the Trenches and into the Future

"Gary Marx has masterfully given us a glimpse of the future in its many aspects, and has also shown us how to prepare to deal with its major challenges."
—*Jack Jennings*, **Founder, Center on Education Policy**

"*Twenty-One Trends for the 21ˢᵗ Century* is a groundbreaking compendium of the most pressing issues that we'll be facing, organized into a highly engaging and accessible book ... a classic example of continuous improvement."
—*Donald Beaudette*, **Associate Professor at Boston University**

"[Marx] lays these many change drivers out and forecasts the specific impacts that they will have on communities, countries, and the entire globe. Then he offers readers suggestions on how they and their organizations can engage with the change processes and stay ahead of the curve."
—*The Futurist* **Magazine, World Future Society**

"Gary Marx is one of the nation's most prominent thinkers about future global trends; informed by his research and work on so many different continents over an extended period of time. In this book, Marx combines traditional research, data analysis, and qualitative interviews to spell out a clear and thoughtful picture of what lies ahead, based upon what is happening and is likely to happen in everything from demographics to energy, leadership to education, and environment to economics."
—*Matthew C. Moen*, **Dean, College of Arts & Sciences, University of South Dakota**

"These trends represent a well-researched, reputable, and reliable source of projections and insights."
—*Avis Glaze*, **President of Edu-quest International, Inc.**

"Gary Marx steers us through the maze of trends that will have a significant impact on our educational leaders, our classrooms, our students and our future. *Twenty-One Trends* offers practical information, ideas and suggestions with the purpose of transforming education, rather than simply defend the status quo."
—*Johnny Veselka*, **Executive Director, Texas Association of School Administrators**

"The 21st Century will look nothing like the last… Buckle up for a wild ride—and make sure you have Marx's book handy to help navigate the challenges."
—*James Harvey*, **Executive Director, National Superintendents Roundtable**

"Marx persuasively calls upon each of us to both think and act together in forming creative solutions that will better address the inevitable problems that arise from rapid systemic changes."
—*Edward Gordon*, **President, Imperial Consulting Corporation, and Author of *Future Jobs***

"The *21 Trends* could be our textbook for ensuring our young people grasp the rapid and profound changes that will impact their lives. We truly need to broaden our curriculum for students so they become global and ethical citizens."
—*Keith Marty*, **Superintendent, Parkway Schools, Chesterfield, Missouri**

A Guide to
Twenty-One Trends
for the
21st Century

Out of the Trenches
and into the Future

Their Profound Implications for Students, Education,
Communities, Countries and the Whole of Society

Gary Marx

EWP **Education Week Press**
Editorial Projects in Education

Library of Congress Cataloging-in-Publication Data
Marx, Gary
A Guide to Twenty-One Trends for the 21st Century: Out of the Trenches and into the Future/Gary Marx
p. cm.
Includes bibliographical references.

A Guide to Twenty-One Trends for the 21st Century (paperback) 978-1-939864-06-2
A Guide to Twenty-One Trends for the 21st Century (ebook) 978-1-939864-07-9

1. EDUCATION/General 2. EDUCATION/Leadership 3. EDUCATION/Professional Development 4. EDUCATION/Research 5. BUSINESS & ECONOMICS/Forecasting

Cover design by Laura Baker & Linda Jurkowitz
Editing and interior design by Jaini Giannovario
Set in Adobe Garamond and Optima LT Std

Education Week Press
6935 Arlington Road
Bethesda, Maryland 20814
www.edweek.org

To order visit: www.edweek.org/go/21trends
Or call 1-800-345-6665. Bulk discounts available.

Views expressed in this publication do not necessarily reflect the opinions or positions of Futures Council 21 or Editorial Projects in Education, Inc.

First Edition 2015, First Printing

To my family, mentors, friends, and colleagues. Thanks for the inspiration, encouragement, and example.

About this Guide to...
Twenty-One Trends for the 21st Century...
Out of the Trenches and into the Future

What we do in the trenches is critical to our future. The danger? Becoming entrenched. We're part of that big world out there, not separate from it. *Twenty-One Trends for the 21st Century* by Gary Marx gets us immediately connected with 21 massive trends that will profoundly impact our future. Call them whatever you'd like: seismic shifts, future forces, an environmental scan, a critical first step in planning, an intelligence report, or an array of strategic insights.

This *Guide*, ideal for distributing to friends, staff, and community, presents only a glimpse of the compelling research you'll find in the primary version of this thoughtful and exciting book. We urge you to also get a copy or copies of that full report for yourself and your organization. If you're an educator, you'll likely want to use it for planning, encouraging futures thinking, as a text for courses or essential reading for professional development, as a gateway for active learning, or just for interesting reading. In it, you'll learn even more about massive trends and their implications for education and the whole of society.

Whatever our walk of life, this *Guide* provides us an opportunity to both enlighten and build on a spirit of leadership for the future. Understanding these forces is essential as we deal with today's challenges and plan for the future. The sense of urgency? Every institution in society is going through an historic reset. No one gets a pass.

TABLE OF CONTENTS

A Guide to Twenty-One Trends for the 21st Century: Out of the Trenches and into the Future

Demographic Sphere

Technology Sphere

Economic Sphere

Energy and Environment Sphere

International/Global Sphere

Education and Learning Sphere

Public and Personal Leadership Sphere

Well-Being Sphere

Introduction

Change is inevitable.
Progress is optional.

> *The question is not, "When will things get back to normal?"*
> *The question is, "What will the new normal look like?"*[1]

Twenty-One Trends for the 21ˢᵗ Century: Out of the Trenches and into the Future is more than a book. It's a living opportunity to get connected to seismic shifts that will profoundly impact our future. No secret to anyone: There's a big world out there, and we *all* need to be part of it. That means we *all* have to *start building. Digging is not enough.*

"We need to address people in the trenches." That's the hue and cry. While the claim is justified by stark daily reality, we'd better make sure we don't dig those trenches so deep that we lose touch with the outside world. In fact, our challenge is to seize higher ground.

Looking at the big picture can open our eyes to strategic perspective and help us better understand the context in which we function. We are, after all, of this world, not separate from it.

Just a Glimpse
Outside the Trenches

This *Guide* provides just a glimpse of 21 massive trends that, in one way or another, have implications for everyone, everywhere. We also recommend that you read the full book, *Twenty-One Trends for the 21ˢᵗ Century*.

Here are just a few examples of handwriting on the wall. We'll briefly explore these and other world-changing realities in the chapters of this book.

• Following every major economic depression or recession, physical and social infrastructure have been transformed, from transportation and manufacturing to lifestyles and education. No one gets a pass.

• Lifelong education will move forward anywhere, anytime, and any way. Similar expectations will impact many other industries.

• While school curriculum will continue to be aligned with goals, pressure will grow for goals to be aligned with individual students' strengths and the needs of society.

• In the U.S., non-Hispanic Whites are expected to fall below 50 percent of the population by about 2043. For those 18 and under—by 2018.

• Beginning in 2011, Baby Boomers started hitting 65 at the rate of about 10,000 a day. They'll be getting to retirement age at 10,000 a day for about 30 years.

• In 2012, members of the Millennial Generation started turning 30 and will be assuming leadership that will be revolutionary for society and our institutions.

• Big data and the cloud, coupled with super- and quantum computers will lead to revolutions in everything from education to health care and raise concerns about identity and privacy. Computer speed and capacity will increase exponentially.

Where are the talented and resourceful people who will help us deal with these massive changes in society? We all know the answer. They're in our schools and colleges today. Think about the 21 trends revealed in this book. Then, answer the question, "What are their implications for education? For students? For communities? For businesses and industries? For government? For nongovernmental organizations? For countries? For the world?"

Dealing with societal trends is an opportunity, as we think about the future, to also demonstrate our *intellectual leadership*, connecting relationships among people, circumstances, and ideas to create new knowledge and inventive solutions to persistent problems. When we confront questions or barriers we need to ask, "What are we going to do about that?" The future won't wait.

What are trends?

The father of issue management, Howard Chase, defined trends as "detectable changes which precede issues."[2]

Webster's Dictionary calls them "a line of general direction or movement, a prevailing tendency or inclination."[3]

Seizing Higher Ground

In a fast changing world, we need perspective. We need to see things in context. That means we must always seek higher ground. All of us have to be ready to deal with life outside the trenches. Unless we stay ahead of the curve, we can expect whole companies, industries, and some other institutions to disappear with the lightening speed of a computer's delete button.

Adaptability and resilience are keys to survival. To freeze is to fail. In every walk of life, all of us are literally facing a choice, knowing that we can only coast downhill. What will it be? Breakthroughs or breakdowns?

Twenty-One Trends is specifically designed to be dynamic, not static—a beginning, not an end in itself. It's a classic environmental scan, shaped to stimulate thinking and provoke discussion. A lifesaver for everyone who does important work in the trenches, it provides an ongoing way to reconnect with the heartbeat of a world in motion.

A bonus for educators is that this book also provides an array of information and processes ideal for engaging students in active learning, project-based education, real-world education, learning across disciplines, learning through inquiry, mastering thinking, reasoning, and problem solving skills, and getting in touch with a highly connected world.

The full version of *Twenty-One Trends*, literally years in the making, can help us move toward higher ground. Think of it as an *intelligence briefing*—as a revealing and invigorating *environmental scan*. As a textbook or required reading, it can energize and stimulate courses or units, professional development programs, community conversations, or Futures Councils. It's a *go-to guide for thinking and planning, a virtual catalog of information and ideas* that will stir possibilities. It's *a key for unlocking rigidity and stimulating ingenuity.* No worries: It's *not* a new program. A commitment to staying in touch is mostly a sign of intellectual rigor and enlightened leadership.

If we understand trends and issues, people say we're *in touch.* If we don't understand trends and issues, they say we're *out of touch.* Being firmly connected to people and ideas is crucial for *each of us* and *all of us.* En Español, *nosotros.*

"An interesting thing happened on the way to accomplishing our plan.
The world changed."

Driving Questions for Educators and Communities

After reviewing trends, ask, "What are the implications of these trends: For how we operate our education system (or organization)? For what students need to know and be able to do…their academic knowledge, skill, attitudes, and behaviors? For economic growth and development and quality of life in our community (or country)?" Of course, anyone can substitute other types of implications they'd like to identify.

**Twenty-One Trends. . . that Will Profoundly Impact Education
and the Whole of Society**

- **Generations:** Millennials will insist on solutions to accumulated problems and injustices and will profoundly impact leadership and lifestyles.
  GIs, Silents, Boomers, Xers → Millennials, Generation E
- **Diversity:** In a series of tipping points, majorities will become minorities, creating ongoing challenges for social cohesion.
  Majority/Minority → Minority/Minority
  Diversity = Division ↔ Diversity = Enrichment   Exclusion ↔ Inclusion
  (**Worldwide:** Growing numbers of people and nations will discover that if we manage our diversity well, it will enrich us. If we don't manage our diversity well, it will divide us.)
- **Aging:** In developed nations, the old will generally outnumber the young. In underdeveloped nations, the young will generally outnumber the old.
  Younger → Older   Older → Younger
- **Technology:** Ubiquitous, interactive technologies will shape how we live, how we learn, how we see ourselves, and how we relate to the world.
  Macro → Micro → Nano → Subatomic   Atoms → Bits
  Megabytes → Gigabytes → Terabytes → Petabytes → Exabytes → Zettabytes (ZB)
- **Identity and Privacy:** Identity and privacy issues will lead to an array of new and often urgent concerns and a demand that they be resolved.
  Knowing Who You Are ↔ Discovering Who Someone Thinks You Are
  What's Private? ↔ What's Not?
- **Economy:** An economy for a new era will demand restoration and reinvention of physical, social, technological, educational, and policy infrastructure.
  Industrial Age Mentality → Global Knowledge/Information Age Reality
  Social and Intellectual Capital → 21ˢᵗ Century Products and Services
- **Jobs and Careers:** Pressure will grow for society to prepare people for jobs and careers that may not currently exist.
  Career Preparation ↔ Employability and Career Adaptability
- **Energy:** The need to develop new sources of affordable and accessible energy will lead to intensified scientific invention and political tension.
  Energy Affordability, Accessibility, Efficiency ↔ Invention,
  Investment, and Political Tension
- **Environmental/Planetary Security:** Common opportunities and threats will intensify a worldwide demand for planetary security.
  Personal Security/Self Interest ↔ Planetary Security
  Common Threats ↔ Common Opportunities
- **Sustainability:** Sustainability will depend on adaptability and resilience in a fast-changing, at-risk world.
  Short-Term Advantage ↔ Long-Term Survival
  Wants of the Present ↔ Needs in the Future

- **International/Global:** International learning, including relationships, cultural understanding, languages, and diplomatic skills, will become basic.
  Isolationist Independence ↔ Interdependence
  (Sub-trend: To earn respect in an interdependent world, nations will be expected to demonstrate their reliability and tolerance.)
- **Personalization:** In a world of diverse talents and aspirations, we will increasingly discover and accept that one size does not fit all.
  Standardization → Personalization
- **Ingenuity:** Releasing ingenuity and stimulating creativity will become primary responsibilities of education and society.
  Information Acquisition → Knowledge Creation and Breakthrough Thinking
- **Depth, Breadth, and Purposes of Education:** The breadth, depth, and purposes of education will constantly be clarified to meet the needs of a fast-changing world.
  Narrowness → Breadth and Depth
- **Polarization:** Polarization and narrowness will, of necessity, bend toward reasoned discussion, evidence, and consideration of varying points of view.
  Narrowness ↔ Open Mindedness   Self Interest ↔ Common Good
- **Authority:** A spotlight will fall on how people gain authority and use it.
  Absolute Authority → Collaboration   Vertical ↔ Horizontal
  Power to Impose ↔ Power to Engage
- **Ethics:** Scientific discoveries and societal realities will force widespread ethical choices.
  Pragmatic/Expedient → Ethical
- **Continuous Improvement:** The status quo will yield to continuous improvement and reasoned progress.
  Quick Fixes/Status Quo → Continuous Improvement
- **Poverty:** Understanding will grow that sustained poverty is expensive, debilitating, and unsettling.
  Sustained Poverty ↔ Opportunity and Hope
- **Scarcity vs. Abundance:** Scarcity will help us rethink our view of abundance.
  Less ↔ More   What's Missing? ↔ What's Possible?
- **Personal Meaning and Work-Life Balance:** More of us will seek personal meaning in our lives in response to an intense, high tech, always on, fast-moving society.
  Personal Accomplishment ↔ Personal Meaning

Trend 1: Generations. *Meet the Future.*

Trend: Millennials will insist on solutions to accumulated problems and injustices and will profoundly impact leadership and lifestyles.

> "**The young do not know enough to be prudent, and therefore they attempt the impossible…and achieve it… generation after generation.**"
> *Pearl Buck*

Generational Milestones
Count the Candles for Boomers and Millennials

Remember 2011? It was an eventful year, but few things could top this headline: *Boomers Hit 65.*[4] How about 2012? As if born of some imagined intergenerational competition, headlines proclaimed, *Millennials Turn 30.*[5] History was being made before our very eyes.

Both of these generational giants had some things in common as they crossed their individual thresholds. One was the Great Recession. Some senior Boomers had to keep working to support their "retirement." At the same time, legions of Millennials were making their way toward center stage, looking for jobs in a tight economy.

History Repeats Itself

How would you like to meet some of the people who will be running the country 40 years from now? "They're already here," says Neil Howe, who with the late William Strauss wrote the seminal book, *Generations.* In it, they traced a parade of generations that have populated our planet for all or parts of six centuries. A generation, they suggest, usually covers a period of 17 to 24 years.[6] One of their most compelling discoveries: *Every fourth generation has a tendency to repeat itself.*[7, 8]

While generations co-exist, each has its uniqueness. Nonetheless, our future depends largely on what we can accomplish together. Generational co-existence is essential.

The Generations
- **G.I. Generation.** Born 1901 to 1924. Often called the "Generation of Heroes."
- **Silent Generation.** Born 1925 to 1945. Smallest generation of the 20th century.
- **Baby Boomers.** Born 1946 to 1964. Largest generation of the 20th century.
- **Generation X.** Born 1965 to 1981. Fewer in number and doubts about the future.
- **Millennial Generation.** Born 1982 to 2003. Moving to center stage.
- **Generation E.** Born 2004-Approx. 2024. May try to cut losses/consolidate gains.

In this chapter, we'll put a spotlight on each of these generations.

Who are we anyway?
GIs, Silents, Boomers, Xers, Millennials, and Es

Consider this a parade of generations. During the next few pages, imagine a drum roll and a bright spotlight that shines on each of these generational groups. When we finish, let's get them all back on stage for a standing ovation. Let our time travel begin!

GI Generation

About 57 million members of the GI Generation were born between 1901 and 1924. At the turn of the 21st century, they were from 76 to 99 years of age. By 2030, when the youngest of this illustrious group will turn 106, we're likely to still have some of them with us. Don't miss the opportunity to get acquainted, listen, and learn.

Widely known as "the generation of heroes," some of them braved two world wars and the Great Depression. Civic minded, they demonstrated a willingness to make huge sacrifices. Members of this generation were shaped by what they considered the common good, and took loyalty, hard work, patriotism, self-reliance, respect for authority, and a strong sense of civic obligation seriously.[9]

GI Generation contemporaries include: John F. Kennedy, Ronald

Reagan, Lyndon Johnson, Thurgood Marshall, George H.W. Bush, Jimmy Carter, Richard Nixon, Gerald Ford, Margaret Thatcher, Louis Armstrong, Bob Hope, Billy Graham, Judy Garland, Frank Sinatra, Hank Williams, Roy Rogers, Lawrence Welk, and Leonard Bernstein.

Silent Generation

Born between 1925 and 1945, the 49 million individuals classified as the Silent Generation make up the smallest generation of the 20th century. In 2010, they were between 65 and 85. By 2030, they'll be from 85 to 105. Their parents, largely members of the GI Generation, hardly ever had a dull moment but did have fewer children as they coped with the Great Depression and World War II. Silents wanted to their souls to have and to give their children a sound home and the security they had yet to experience.

Silents are generally known for patriotism, hard work, willingness to sacrifice, patience, honor, loyalty, and varying levels of conformity. It's a generation that never had a U.S. president, but its outer conformity camouflaged an intense dedication to purpose, sparked waves of creative genius, and led a civil rights revolution.

Silents' contemporaries include or once included people like Martin Luther King, Jr., Neil Armstrong, Elvis Presley, The Beatles, James Brown, Tony Bennett, Bob Dylan, Ray Charles, Willie Nelson, Sammy Davis, Jr., Quincy Jones, Jimi Hendrix, Buddy Holly, Aretha Franklin, Patsy Cline, Dick Clark, Johnny Carson, Steve Martin, Jackie Kennedy, Muhammad Ali, Marilyn Monroe, Anne Frank, Carl Sagan, Colin Powell, Robert and Ted Kennedy, Che Guevara, Pope Francis, and Queen Elizabeth.

Baby Boomers

Born between 1946 and 1964, Boomers, something like 79 million strong, were, up to that time, the largest generation ever produced by the United States... with counterparts in other countries. Theirs was the first generation of the century not to have experienced a world war or the Great Depression. Their parents hailed largely from the Silent and GI Generations. Boomers experienced the impact of television,

Vietnam, and Woodstock.

By 2030, Boomers will be between 66 and 84, and we'll have only about two people of "working age" for every person drawing benefits from Social Security. Moving ahead to 2050, Boomers will be from 86 to 104.

Contemporaries of Boomers include: Barack and Michelle Obama, George W. and Laura Bush, Bill and Hillary Clinton, John Kerry, Princess Diana of Wales, Bill Gates, Steve Jobs, Jeff Bezos, Steven Spielberg, Oprah Winfrey, Dolly Parton, Bruce Springsteen, Michael Jackson, Tom Hanks, Denzel Washington, Stevie Wonder, George Clooney, and Prince Charles.

Generation X

Born during the Baby Bust of 1965 and 1981, the estimated 51 million Xers were sandwiched between the more or less gigantic Boomers and Millennials. Xers have dazzled the world with a kind of low-key genius. In 2010, Xers were between 29 and 45. In 2030, their birthday cakes will blaze with anywhere from 49 to 65 candles and in 2050, from 69 to 85. Only those who live to be 119 will see 2100. It might just happen.

Xers developed the traits of free agents, such as being self-reliant, independent, individualistic, resilient, adaptable, and entrepreneurial. As the economy changed, they often saw their parents laid off or face job insecurity. In response to that experience, some Xers gave up on the idea of loyalty to a single organization.

Xer contemporaries include: David Cameron, Michael Dell, Tiger Woods, Jimmy Fallon, Reese Witherspoon, Jennifer Lopez, Jennifer Hudson, Ben Stiller, Mike Tyson, Peyton and Eli Manning, Julia Roberts, Kobe Bryant, Yao Ming, Shaquille O'Neal, Lance Armstrong, Tupac Shakur, Eminem, Christina Aguilera, and Britney Spears.

The Millennials

Born between 1982 and about 2003, the 76 million U.S. Millennials outnumbered most of the generations that came before them. They are the fourth generation out from the GI Generation, and in a 21st century way, share a number of their motivations. People who really listen to them tell us that this is a generation with high aspirations for themselves, particularly focused on dealing with longstanding problems and injustices.

In 2010, members of the Millennial Generation were between 7 and 28. In 2012, the first of them celebrated their 30th. By 2030, they'll be from 27 to 48. By then, they will likely hold down a growing number of key political positions. Move ahead to 2050 and our Millennials will be in prime time, from 47 to 68. The eldest of them will turn 100 in 2082 and the youngest in 2103.

While each member of this ubiquitous, tech-savvy generation is unique, a common portrait includes: optimism, focus, high personal expectations, a sense of enormous academic pressure, digital literacy that grew from never knowing a world without computers, unlimited access to information and connections, comfort with teamwork, and seeing the world as a place that's open 24/7.

By the way, not everyone calls them Millennials. They are alternately known as: Generation Y, the Echo Boomers, Gen Tech, Generation Text, Dot Com, Nexters, and the Net Generation. Who are some of the better-known Millennials? The list of those who are known on the world stage is growing. Some include: Princes William and Harry, Duchess of Cambridge Kate Middleton, Mark Zuckerberg, Taylor Swift, Adele, Justin Bieber, Lady Gaga, LeBron James, Danica Patrick, Carrie Underwood, and Malala Yousafzai. Feel free to add to this list.

What Else Do We Need to Know about Millennials?
Leaders in the Making

For anyone else concerned about shaping the future, including educators, here are a few other things about this formative generation that we may want to consider.

Scores of Millennials have taken their values to the streets and to the ballot box as they pursue a belief that the status quo will not cut it—that vertical, top down decision-making needs to become more collaborative. They sparked the Arab Spring.

Convergence is emerging as the name of the game. Growing polarization is both a turn-off and a turn-on—a turn off for politics as usual and a turn on for finding a better way.

Many Millennials, looking for a place to live, are taking a close look at the cost of lifestyle, earnings, vitality, after hours life, learning opportunities, ease in getting around town, diversity, low crime rates, opportunities for civic engagement, and answers to long commute times, such as mass transit, or ideally walk- or bike-ability.[10] With a perfect storm of yet-to-be-paid college loans, higher prices for a place to live, and job scarcity, growing numbers were going urban and upsizing by downsizing.

In teaching a hyper-tech-savvy generation of students, we should not forget the importance of content along with interaction. Thinking, reasoning, problem solving, creativity, entrepreneurial, and communication skills, coupled with ethical behavior, will be essential if we hope to even have a future. As we teach everything from STEM to social studies, civic education, and the arts, we generally need to align with revolutionary changes in how new generations of students get and process information.

Like it or not, Lauren Friese and Cassandra Jowett of TalentEgg (talentegg.ca), writing for Canada's *Globe and Mail*, tell us that Millennials will transform how we work. Look for more instant messaging, less email, fewer pointless or redundant meetings, more "immediate, effective feedback," and ROWE, "the results-only workplace."[11]

Generation E...for Equilibrium

Just as the Silents followed the GI Generation, it's likely something akin to Generation E will follow on the heels of the Millennials. E, in this case, stands for equilibrium. Members of this new generation will likely be born between 2004 and 2024. That assumes a 20-year generation, which may be a stretch. If that assumption holds, the youngest will celebrate a 76th and the oldest a 96th birthday in 2100.

We might expect the Es to spawn a new era for politics and world affairs, education, and numerous other field of human endeavor. For this largely 21st century generation, problem solving skills and futures studies will likely be firmly placed on the list of basics. As for technologies, they will increasingly become nearly invisible as people think of them not necessarily as tools but as extensions of their minds and bodies. Like the Silents four generations before them, they will probably break through any conformity that may have developed to create a whole new era of arts and culture, which, today, is only at the edges of our imaginations.

High on their generational agendas will be a commitment *to cutting our losses and consolidating our gains* and perhaps settling, even for a very short time, on what we might call a *21st century version of a new normal.*

> "A small body of determined spirits fired by an unquench-
> able faith in their mission can alter the course of history."
> *Mahatma Gandhi[12]*

Implications for Education and Society—*Generations*

The flow of generations has profound implications for every education system and every society in the world. For example, Millennials will generally be committed to solving problems and dealing with injustices. They will need to understand how to resolve disputes peacefully and democratically, if we hope to avoid unthinkable destruction. As polarized politicians "kick the can down the road," failing to make critical decisions that will affect multiple generations, Millennials and Generation E will need to add their unfinished business and the cost of neglect to other urgent issues they will face. By the way, expect members of these generations to be a decisive force in political campaigns, and advocates for individual and human rights as well as education.

Communities and countries will be pressed to provide reasonable employment opportunities, support for entrepreneurship, infrastructure, and a compelling quality of life. All are keys to attracting and keeping well-educated young people. Implications?

• **Building intergenerational relationships and communication skills.** Deliberately orchestrating multi-generational teams, planning sessions, cross-generational mentoring, and professional development can build relationships and add to our wisdom.

• **Teaching students how to make change peacefully and democratically.** As Millennials move into positions of leadership, they will confront longstanding problems and injustices and demand that they be resolved. To deal with issues of this magnitude, they will need a broad understanding of history, culture, and human behavior, as well as thinking, reasoning, and problem solving skills.

• **Listening to students . . . giving them a voice. Getting them engaged.** Animated, energetic, committed generations of students will expect their voices to be heard in decisions that affect their education and their individual and collective futures. And it is *their* future.

• **Building media literacy skills.** As generations of all ages attempt to take on community or world problems, they will need to be armed with media literacy skills. How else will they be able to separate truth from fiction or opinion, wheat from chaff, legitimate information from disinformation?

• **Preparing students for realities of the 21ˢᵗ century workplace.** Whether they aspire to work locally or globally, each needs to be prepared for rigor, self-discipline, languages, teamwork, an eagerness for feedback, and a demand for results in the *real world*. That will mean effective face-to-face and online communication and thoughtful relationships across generations.

Trend 2. Diversity. *E Pluribus Unum*

Trend: In a series of tipping points, majorities will become minorities, creating ongoing challenges for social cohesion.

> **"The U.S. will become the first major post-industrial society in the world where minorities will be the majority."**
> *Marcello Suárez-Orozco[13]*

E Pluribus Unum

It's the U.S. motto, "Of the Many… One," but it is much more. It is a statement of belief that people of every shape, size, shade, and belief can work together to build a civil society, a sustainable environment, and a viable economy. While we're working together, we can also pursue our own individual dreams.

Now, wherever we live on the planet, we are faced with this stark reality: If we manage our diversity well, it will enrich us. If we don't manage it well, it will divide us. Meeting that challenge is up to each of us and all of us.

Majority Becomes Minority
We're in the midst of a seismic shift!

Get ready. It will likely happen between 2040 and 2050. If projections hold true, every racial or ethnic group will, in essence, become a minority by about 2043. In fact, tipping points for the trend got underway in 2011.

Tipping Points, a Minority/Minority Society… By Age Group. Brookings Institution Demographer William Frey interpreted December 2012 U.S. Census Bureau projections. He pointed out, by age group, when non-Hispanic Whites are likely to become less than 50 percent of the U.S. population. *Total Population*: 2043, *Age 1*: 2011, *Age 5*: 2013-14, *Under Age 18*: 2018, *Ages 18-29*: 2027, *Ages 30-44*:

2035, *Ages 45-64:* 2051, *Ages 65+:* After 2060 [14] [15] Of course, this situation begs the question: What do you call majorities when they become minorities… or minorities when they become majorities?

> **"I have a dream that one day, on the red hills of Georgia, the sons of former slaves and the sons of former slave owners will sit down at the table of brotherhood. I have a dream today."**
> *Martin Luther King, Jr., 1963*

Exclusion vs. Inclusion, The Danger of Dominance

When domination by one or more groups replaces an acceptance of diversity as the norm, people generally engage in conflicts that involve: tribal, racial, and ethnic divisions; religious differences; and a variety of other social and economic divides. Without some sense of democratic inclusiveness, people who identify with divergent groups will either feel "in power" or "out of power."

How Did We Get So Diverse?

One answer to that question is immigration. The other is the stork—or birth rates. Those are among the forces impacting population diversity in many parts of the world. Educators know that the ebb and flow can make a big difference in who shows up for school next year.

Immigration… The Road to Diversity. We live in an age of massive migration, as people cross political boundaries and oceans to pursue what they hope will be an opportunity to pursue their futures. Refinements in immigration policy require constant adjustments to keep them in line with social and economic realities.

Worldwide, *more-developed countries* generally have declining or very slowly increasing populations. Among exceptions are the U.S., Canada, and Mexico, which are expected to show steady gains, at least through 2100.[16] A prime reason for the U.S. population increase is immigration and the children of immigrants.

In 2011, traditional minorities had become more than 50 percent of the population in U.S. states or equivalents, such as: Hawaii (77.1 percent), District of Columbia (64.7 percent), California (60.3 percent), New Mexico (59.8 percent), and Texas (55.2 percent).[17]

A Level Playing Field. Perhaps no mantra has echoed so long as, "We need to improve minority student achievement." We sometimes call it "equal educational opportunity for *all*," or the need for "a level playing field for all." Whatever we call it, the sense of urgency keeps growing. An *inclusive identity* and *teaching membership and belonging* are essential. Futures Council 21 member Michael Usdan calls for reassurance that "equality of opportunity" will be "more than empty rhetoric for growing numbers of youngsters."

What is Social Cohesion?
In essence, it's the glue that holds us together…as families, as nations, as a world. What we have in common helps us form our sense of community.

Implications for Education and Society—*Diversity*

We are moving at deliberate speed from a majority/minority to a minority/minority society. That reality has substantial implications for our individual and collective futures.

• **Getting ready for a minority/minority society.** If *exclusion* or *exclusive* has ever been part of the equation, it needs to be adjusted in the direction of *inclusion* and *inclusive*. Students, educators, parents, and communities need to understand and celebrate our combinations of diversities and the fact that we are all in the same boat.

• **Ensuring equal opportunity and improving achievement for** *all* **students. Raising all boats.** Our education systems exist in a complex and exciting time of mass migration and accelerating demographic change. That means increased diversity, including race, ethnicity, national origin, gender identity, sexual orientation, age, disabilities, political, religious, language, marital status, life experiences, and more. Perhaps no other issue raised by this trend is more critical than making sure each and every student has an equal opportunity to receive a sound education.

• **Providing inclusive education that reflects a world of diversity.** From the largest metropolitan area to the smallest rural community, all of our students (all of *us*) will have to survive and thrive in a world of multiple cultures, made even smaller by instant communication and rapid transportation. If we cut ourselves off or sell our students short, the world will simply pass us by.

• **Renewing our identities, seeking common denominators, and working toward social cohesion.** A 20th century identity may not be sustainable in a 21st century world. That means helping our countries, communities, schools, colleges, staff, and students understand and embrace an identity that reflects evolving demographics and the changing face of the nation and world. It might also mean that we need to consider constantly renewing our curriculum and instruction to make sure that they are inclusive.

• **Recognizing the high cost of exclusion.** Communities, countries, and the world have too often overtly or just by default marginalized people who were different from themselves. Without inclusion, enclaves can develop, what South African teacher Jessica Vinod Kumar sometimes calls "social cacooning." The overall, society-wide, long-term, unspoken, most expensive item in most budgets or economies could very well be the high cost of neglect.

• **Maintaining high expectations for *all* and the resources to pursue them.** Educators and communities need to be talent scouts, searching for talents, interests, abilities, and aspirations among *all* children and adults. Then, they need to focus on helping them grow and develop.

• **Developing an international focus, cultural sensitivity, language, and other communication skills.** The student who is prepared for the future will need a grounding not just in the pop culture of his or her own country but in the histories, cultures, people, and languages of the world. Multiple languages will be expected. All students, wherever they live, need a global perspective. In the U.S., English Language Learning (ELL) programs should be considered essential.

• **Additional Implications.** Schools and colleges will need to attract diverse, talented members of the team as both excellent educators and role models. Preparation and professional development programs at all levels should address diversity and inclusion. Culturally sensitive communication will be essential in building understanding within the school or college and throughout the community. Inclusive leadership should aim for a spirit of—*We're all in this together.*

Trend 3: Aging. *We're living longer. Ready for 100?*

Trend: In developed nations, the old will generally outnumber the young. In developing nations, the young will generally outnumber the old.

|| **"Old age isn't so bad when you consider the alternative."**[18]
|| *Maurice Chevalier, French actor, singer, and showman*

Aging: We Can Live with It!

If we're lucky enough, it happens to all of us. We get older. We add to our life experience and, if we have reasonably good health, get bonus time to enjoy our families, nature, and life itself. Some even tell us that, along the way, we become wise.

Globally, in more developed parts of the world, people, on average, are getting considerably older. When that happens, populations tend to drop. At the same time, developing nations are, on average, getting younger. Their populations are skyrocketing. That contrast will fuel seismic shifts—socially, economically, and politically.

Make way for a rising tide of issues firmly rooted in aging. On the home front, the solvency of pension funds, the cost and availability of health services, and a host of other concerns have taken center stage as Baby Boomers reach retirement age at the rate of 10,000 a day until about 2030.

The Handwriting Is On The Wall:

In 2000, when the U.S. population was 282 million—
27 percent were 18 or younger—21 percent were 55 or older.

Moving ahead to 2030, when the U.S. population will be about 358 million and the Baby Boom Generation will be between 66 and 84 years of age—
22 percent will be 18 or younger—and 31 percent will be 55 or older.[19]

Six Key Factors that Impact Aging

Life Expectancies. In 2010, the average U.S. life expectancy had climbed to 78.2 years, ranking approximately 51st among nations of the world.[20] The country is expected to have a life expectancy of 83 by 2030.

Median Ages. In *1850*, the *average age* of people in the United States was 19.[21] Remarkably, the average doubled to about 36.5 years by 2000. The *median age*, midpoint between older and younger, increased to 37.2 in 2010. By 2050, it's expected to reach 38.8 and possibly 40.3 in 2100.[22]

Birth Rates. While life expectancies and median ages continue their relentless climb, U.S. birth rates have taken a steady nosedive. In *1910*, the United States registered 3.01 *live births per 100 population*. In *1960*, there were 2.37. By *1990*, the rate had fallen to 1.67[23] and in *2010* dropped even further to 1.30.[24] *Basic replacement rate is 2.1.*

Fertility Rates. While *birth rates* reveal the number of *live births per 100 population, fertility rates* reflect the *average number of live births per 100 women of normal childbearing age, 15 to 44*. Historically, the numbers of children we conceive tends to drop as education levels rise or as economies improve. Fertility rates in the U.S. have continued on a downward trajectory, reaching 6.32 in 2011 in the midst of the Great Recession, compared to 12.68 in 1910.[25]

Death Rates. Of course, death rates play a key role in the shift toward an aging population. In 2010, the United States reported 8.0 deaths per 1,000 population,[26] compared to 14.7 in 1910.[27] Death rates are projected to remain stable at about 8. In 2025, expect a slight uptick to about 9.[28]

Immigration. A population factor that ameliorates the effect of all others is immigration—and it's having a profound impact on the very face of the planet. It is a known fact that millions of people will use any means available to pursue opportunity—the chance for education, economic advancement, and the freedom to fulfill their dreams.

A Few More Facts about Aging

U.S. Population Growth. The population of the United States is expected to grow from 281.4 million in 2000 to approximately 399.8

million in 2050. During that time, the massive 79 million strong Baby Boomers will move into their advanced years. In 1950, 12.7 million people were 65 or older. In 2010, it was 40.4 million.

Social Security. The Social Security Administration (SSA) is expecting to have only 2.1 people working for every beneficiary by 2030. That compares with 16 people working for every person drawing benefits in 1950. A few more facts for perspective: U.S. life expectancy in 1950 was 68.2 years. In 2010, it had risen to 78.2.[29] That's more years in retirement. While people who make products for mature consumers are salivating, those working to keep Social Security, Medicare, and Medicaid solvent are burning the midnight oil.

World Population Growth. Earth's population was about 2.5 billion in 1950. By 2000, it had reached 6.08 billion. International experts are projecting a world population of 7.62 billion by 2020 and 9.0 billion-plus by 2050. That's a 3.6 times increase from 1950 to 2050.[30]

In the *more developed world*, youth populations tend to be dropping and people are living longer. Where will they get fresh people for the work force? Who will support their pension plans? By contrast, in the *developing world*, nations are seeing massive increases in their youth populations but have few people older than 55. A persistent shortfall in education, jobs, and other opportunities can lead to anger, unrest, continuous chaos, revolution, civil wars, or even international terrorism.

Aging in Education. Here's the rub. At the same time enrollments in schools and colleges continue to go up, Baby Boom teachers are moving into retirement.

Enrollments in U.S. public and private K-12 schools are expected to increase from 54.7 million in 2010 to 57.94 million in 2020.[31] In 2010, approximately 20.58 million students attended *postsecondary degree-granting institutions*. Those schools were projected to enroll approximately 23.01 million by 2020.[32]

Aging, Health, and Longevity. In October 2009, *ABC News* quoted an article in the medical journal, *The Lancet,* showing that, "based on current trajectories, more than half of all babies born in industrialized nations since the year 2000 can expect to live into triple digits." Dr. Kaare Christensen, a Danish epidemiologist, observed, "If you're going to retire when you are 60 or 65, it looks quite different when your life expectancy is 75 or 80 than when it's 100."[33]

Implications for Education and Society—*Aging*

The impact of aging on society will be massive. As the U.S. entered the second decade of the 21st century, nearly 40 million people were 65 or older, about 13 percent of the population. That number was expected to reach between 80 and 90 million by 2050, around 20 percent of the population.[34]

It's a cinch that political, economic, social, and technological concerns will multiply as the nation honors, cares for, continues to educate, technologically connects, and taps the talents of unprecedented numbers of older people.

We can expect pension programs to be strained to their limits as the ratio of retirees closes in on the number of actual workers contributing to those funds. Pressure will grow to extend the viability of programs such as Social Security, Medicare, and Medicaid. The need and expectations for medical care will intensify. Research will continue in development of life extension sciences. Communities will be pressed to plan ahead for quality geriatric medical and day care, assisted living, nursing homes, and other services for an aging population.

With massive retirements, several nations will be effectively losing a base of experience and a level of talent that may be difficult to replace. Demand will accelerate for products and services directly related to the needs and wants of older citizens, many with substantial buying power. Here are a few more implications of aging.

• **Maintaining an education workforce.** As enrollments increase, growing numbers of Boomer educators will retire. Concerns have flourished about the need to make education careers more attractive to younger generations and retain more of the talent that is already there. Many seasoned retirees will continue to fill needs and gaps.

• **Expanding career education, adult education, community and four-year college and university programs, and other opportunities for lifelong learning.** The K-12 system may not cover enough ground to meet the expanding needs of older citizens who are looking for new later-in-life careers, trying to satisfy their intellectual curiosities, or upgrading their technology/computer skills. Many schools already offer their own community/adult/continuous education programs. A variety of online courses bring learning to students, including older citizens, anytime and anywhere.

• **Promoting cross-generational communication.** Society is faced with providing services across all or parts of five generations. At the same time, schools and colleges will be considering how to prepare students for intergenerational understanding—an essential for maintaining a civil society.

• **Communicating and collaborating with people who don't have kids in school.** One question that crops up frequently within the education system at all levels is, "How can we inform, engage, and serve people who don't have kids in our schools?"

• **Balancing political demands of the young and the old.** Educators of children and young adults will appeal for funding and support to prepare students for a fast-changing world. At the same time, growing numbers of retiring Boomers will demand services for older citizens.

• **Maintaining public assistance for low-income seniors.** Many communities will see a growing demand for public assistance from older people whose home values and nest-eggs may have dropped and jobs disappeared. Their energy, food, pharmaceuticals, and other essentials will likely continue to be more expensive.

• **Creating more industries serving older citizens.** As average ages go up and people live longer, look for new products and services to serve their needs. From food services, transportation, and assistive devices to geriatric day care, assisted living, and continuing education, demographics will create opportunities for service, whole new industries, and jobs.

• **Embracing active seniors.** Look for growing numbers of seniors who will take time to vote and be a significant force in elections. Get ready for the creation of new consultancies that allow seasoned people to share their experiences and advice. Be prepared for older citizens to stay on the job longer, if at all possible, and to work part time. Expect a growing demand for financial, travel, and fitness services.

Trend 4: Technology.
Flash Gordon to Flash Drives

Trend: Ubiquitous, interactive technology will shape how we live, how we learn, how we see ourselves, and how we relate to the world.

> **"Computer wins on Jeopardy!"**[35]
> *New York Times, February 16, 2011*

Ever wonder how it feels to live during a revolution? Well, look around and take a deep breath. It's happening again. It's a technological revolution that is pushing us forward at a speed that tests our adaptability, ingenuity, patience, and even our budgets as we try to keep up with the Joneses and stay ahead of the curve.

Changes have become exponential. Convergence, miniaturization, speed, memory, power, connectivity, and price are the name of the game. Emerging technologies take us beyond what most of us would even have imagined only a few decades ago. We carry a world of information and worldwide connections in our pocket or purse. The startling part is that what we see is only the beginning of what's to come. The good news? We can use that technology to help us shape the future rather than just go along for the ride.

Social networking sites such as Facebook, Twitter, Pinterest, Instagram, Skype, Tumblr, Snapchat, Reddit, and just plain email have put us in instant contact with each other across political, social, economic, and other boundaries. Each of us can originate our own network, share ideas in the blogosphere, get involved in a chat, meet-up, conduct and exchange research, and do *crowdsourcing* or *mass mobbing*. Futures Council 21 member Ryan Hunter points out his generation's ease in "facilitating creation and engagement of an online kind of civil society quite literally at their fingertips."

Online courses or "blended learning" have become commonplace. Virtual and augmented reality can take us there without actually being there.

Hand-held, wireless, even wearable communication devices have become an extension of our bodies and minds, sources of what seem like an unlimited array of information and connections. There is an app for nearly everything, packed into a multiplying number of devices. In essence, miraculous gadgets create a ubiquitous worldwide town square.

A veteran superintendent of the Howard–Suamico Public Schools in Green Bay, Wisconsin, Damian LaCroix remarks, "We can't educate today's students for tomorrow's challenges with yesterday's schools." He sees "the proliferation of technology flipping the traditional 20th century model of education and transforming it into a new digital high-tech, high-touch landscape."

"It is difficult to say what is impossible, for the dream of yesterday is the hope of today and the reality of tomorrow."
Robert Goddard

Flash Gordon to Flash Drives

Blame the comic books and strips, moviemakers, television producers, and science fiction writers, if you'd like. Flash Gordon, Buck Rogers, and Star Trek piqued our imaginations. They left an impression that nearly anything is possible.

Byte-Size. With dizzying speed, we have raced from megabytes to gigabytes, terabytes, and petabytes. What comes next for computer power? By the time you read this, we might be zipping into exabytes and zettabytes, to say nothing of *yottabytes* and *kibibytes*. When it comes to computer speed and capacity, we are soaring beyond the known universe.

Big Data and the Cloud. It may sound like the name of a 1960s rock group, but, in the technology world, they are a big deal. *Big data*, for example, is basically a term used to describe the massive amounts of information we are accumulating, "growing at 50 percent a year, or more than doubling every two years." Big data analysts are needed to help companies use that information to develop marketing plans, design cars, stock store shelves, and help politicians shape their messages.[36]

Cloud computing is a web-based service offered by companies that have picked it up as a business model. Using clusters of computers, they take care of everything from email and word processing to data analytics. Those companies that offer cloud services must store your data in two different places, just in case of a gigantic glitch. Many of us end up connecting to the cloud, especially if we use certain web-based email services.[37] The cloud, by the way, is often the home of big data.

> **"Technology will become the great equalizer across the globe, giving access to education, knowledge, and wealth, to even more people."**
> *Sheldon Berman, Superintendent of Schools, Eugene, Oregon*

The Nano Scale. We may have started with macro, but since then, we've gone from small to tiny, from microscopic and submicroscopic to subatomic. We're now able to work on the nanoscale. That is, indeed, small, or short for that matter—a *nanometer* is one-billionth of a meter; a *nanosecond* is one-billionth of a second.

Nanotechnology gives us the ability to manipulate atoms and molecules, promising stronger, lighter-weight materials than the world has ever known, faster computers, unprecedented medical breakthroughs, and atomically precise molecular manufacturing. Eric Drexler, who heads the Foresight Institute, looks toward "desktop computers with one billion processors…and materials 100 times stronger than steel."[38]

Super Computers. Moore's Law is interpreted to mean that computer power will double every 18 months. Justin Rattner, Chief Technology Officer at Intel Corporation, the world's largest maker of superconductors,[39] says, "Science and technology have progressed to the point where what we build is only constrained by the limits of our imagination."

What does it take to be called a "supercomputer?" While definitions might vary, one that seems to have fairly widespread application is—anything that is much more powerful than what we commonly use today. For example, 20 years ago, your present PC, tablet, smartphone, or other device may very well have been considered a supercomputer.

A Quantum Computer. As we reach the limits of silicon chips, quantum computers will likely "encode data in the quantum states of subatomic particles known as quantum bits—or qubits."[40] The stakes are high since the power, speed, and analytic ability of these computers will be off the charts. Welcome to the subatomic world.

Universal Service. We are now connected to an information superhighway. However, a clear challenge is *universal service* and a need to ensure that high-speed Internet connections are available to everyone, wherever they are. Progress in the economy and civil society as well as a commitment to a level playing field are all at stake.

Upsides and Downsides. We've learned the hard way that any technology, from gunpowder to computer power, can have both an upside and a downside.

A smartphone, with its digital camera, can capture memorable family photos. It can also rally people for a noble cause or instruct them in carrying out an act of violence. Hacking, data piracy, and cyberbullying get constant headlines. Technologies that can put us in contact with the world and serve as revolutionary education tools can also become addictive, depriving us of in-person social interaction.

The World of Technology

In a world of technology that seems to be developing on steroids, much more is yet to come. Consider the industries, professions, careers, and jobs that flow from each one. In the meantime, here are highlights from a few fields:

Medical technologies have generally improved the ability of medical doctors to diagnose and treat ailments (or rule them out).

Robotics is expanding exponentially. Robots have been used to automate factories, explore the surface of Mars, conduct dangerous searches for victims of disasters, operate in combat zones, assist in medical care, and even deliver packages.

Printing and imaging are going through a revolution. Formats from very small to very large are a product of that revolution, which makes it possible for marketers, communicators, and merchants to target increasingly smaller and more diverse sub-groups.[41] *3D printing,* sometimes called desktop or additive manufacturing, can be pre-programmed to produce three-dimensional items ranging from prototypes to a jawbone, an auto part, a gun, or something you see in an animated movie.

Quantum mechanics and particle physics, coupled with nanotechnology, allow us to move atoms around inside the molecule. Powerful microscopes help us to look *in* while new generations of telescopes help us look *out* into intergalactic space. Voyager and Pioneer probes are now cruising outside our solar system. We have rovers on Mars, and we're discovering exoplanets. Space tourism is becoming a reality, but tickets will be expensive and you'll have to pack light. Let's hope it will all dazzle student imaginations, and lure even more of them into astrophysics, bioinformatics, and nanotechnology.

> **The increasing ubiquitousness of technology—what today is considered of interest will tomorrow be a given. Technology immigrants think about technology. For digital natives, children and young adults, technology just is.**
> *Stephen Murley, superintendent, Iowa City School District, Iowa City, Iowa*

How Educators are Using Technologies
A Few Examples

New technologies are enlivening schools and colleges. Many are putting them to creative use to enhance student learning. Some are using an array of devices, programs, and apps to do more efficiently what they have always done.

Others are coupling these new technologies with professional development and adjustments in mentalities about the physical set-ups of classrooms long reminiscent of the Industrial Age. Software is out there to flag us if a student is falling behind, to help students capture and play back lecture notes, and to build comprehension skills.[42]

Are we ready for on-demand, constantly-updated curriculum, available 24-7? What are the benefits? What are the challenges and side effects? What are the limitations? Will we see schools and classrooms differently? How are some schools and colleges using these tools to enhance our ongoing need for truly educated people?

Immersive Technology. From his post at the Harvard Graduate School of Education, Chris Dede describes an "immersive learning environment," reinforced with an array of technologies. Students go to a pond, and aided by their smartphones and iPads, they find connections to explain what they are experiencing with water quality, fish, and other plant and wildlife. Dede sees students "developing an understanding of complex causal relationships" and doing science "the way science is done."[43]

MOOCs. Massively Open Online Courses, which are increasingly common among postsecondary schools, offer online access to learning. Often included are readings, videos, and other possibilities for learning, all on a technology platform. A concern is that student results might be tough to monitor and income streams could be scarce.

An Array of Possibilities. Many schools are using tablet computers loaded with interactive e-textbooks, artwork, and videos to help explain concepts, as well as (sometimes filtered) connections to the Internet. Virtual schools allow students to take online courses that may not be offered in their home schools, complete with interactive games, virtual field trips, and video lessons that can help reinforce certain subjects. Artificial intelligence (AI) and augmented reality (AR) can be part of the mix. Education systems often provide a special online site for students and parents to stay up to date on schedules, assignments, courses, and other information. Futures Council member Gary Rowe observes, "Technologies will continue to disrupt traditional school models," based on just "doing school."

> **"Blended learning will result in the need for extensive changes in how teachers teach and how a student wishes to learn."**
> *Marcus Newsome, superintendent, Chesterfield County Public Schools, Virginia*

Implications for Education and Society—*Technology*

Implications of the technology trend are as ubiquitous as the technology itself.

Career and job opportunities in technology-related for-profit and not-for-profit industries will increase dramatically, amplifying pressure to educate qualified people.

Not only are new technologies developing at an exponential pace but they are unrelenting as we reshape our education system and deal with their impact on the whole of society. Here are a few of those implications:

• **Getting, Employing, Maintaining, and Constantly Updating Technologies.** The tools of technology, such as laptops, tablets, smartphones, and other interactive devices, plus the programs and apps that bring them to life, have become indispensible and pervasive tools for education. From instruction and assessment to administration, budgeting, scheduling, and communication to making strategic decisions, all education systems need to move forward. There is no going back. Keep this in mind: In 2012, around three-quarters of the world's inhabitants had access to a mobile phone.[44]

• **Ensuring Constantly Renewed Learning Materials in a Fast-Changing World.** While textbooks have significant value, some education systems are supplementing them with *techbooks* that offer connections to constantly updated information as well as videos and a variety of apps to enhance learning.

• **Becoming Facilitators and Orchestrators of Learning.** As concertmasters, teachers will increasingly turn the process of teaching and learning into a partnership, with students and teachers constantly learning from each other. Self-learning will be seen as a bonus—and encouraged.

• **Considering How Education is Delivered.** Schools and colleges have growing alternatives for delivering education. Choices range from presentations and discussions in the classroom to online, blended, and hybrid courses. Flipping has become either a stated or unstated practice in some schools, with students watching something like a lecture online so that in-class time can be used for various learning activities. Futurist John Meagher foresees "the rise of virtual universities where the greatest minds are on tap," with "open-access to students in third world nations, and in poor areas of the U.S."

• **Enhancing Personalization, Reinforcement, and Research.** Like a violin in the hands of a master, various technologies can help us personalize education, deliver instruction, monitor what students have learned and where they need help, provide reinforcement, make inter-active assignments, and serve as tools to conduct research. Students can prepare papers or presentations using video, audio, Skype, and Power-Point, do assessments of their progress, and seek help.

• **Strengthening Media Literacy Skills, Preparing Students for Appropriate Use of Social Media.** Since students, all of us for that matter, are virtually bombarded with information and enticements to grab our attention, media literacy skills have become more important than ever. We need to be quite clear about how we are teaching students to separate wheat from chaff, truth from fiction. Of course, ethical use of media, etiquette (netiquette), and solid approaches for dealing with cyberbullying are essential.

All classrooms must have wireless Internet capabilities, computers for all to use, and handheld devices for research and transmitting schoolwork.
Rebecca Mieliwocki, 2012 U.S. National Teacher of the Year, Luther Burbank Middle School, Burbank, California

• **Reinforcing Face-to-Face Communication, Dealing with Technology Addiction.** Varying clusters of technologies can become so captivating, in some cases so addictive, that people may need les-sons for interpersonal, face-to-face communication and breaking any cyber-addictions. While online activities can be enlightening and help build relationships, they can also turn into obsessive Internet disorders.

• **Promoting Two-Way, Interactive Communication.** Schools and colleges may still have printed newsletters and other publications, but they also have web sites. They connect on Facebook, Twitter, My Space, Tumbler, Chatterkick, Reddit, and through other social media, such as email. They post video on YouTube; share something you might like on Pinterest; do blogs, and get involved in chat rooms. Security threats and weather emergencies are delivered online.

Trend 5: Identity and Privacy.
Life is an open book.

Trend: Identity and privacy issues will lead to an array of new and often urgent concerns and a demand that they be resolved.

> **"Just because you're paranoid doesn't mean that they aren't after you."**
> *Joseph Heller, Catch-22*[45]

Reputation Analysis…Who am I?

Part 1: If you ask people you know to describe you, what words would they use?

Part 2: What words would you like them to use?

Part 3: Note the gap and consider what you might do about it, if anything.

Our "big data identity," stored in the cloud and captured by data mining sources such as cookies and Trojan horses, will likely be based on the demographics of our zip code; our age, race, or ethnicity; whether we have children; our political leanings; our affiliations; and where we shop. It will likely reflect the types of foods we buy, the age and make of our car, the clothes we wear, the movies we've seen, the music we've downloaded, the pictures we've placed on *Facebook*, our medical records, pharmaceuticals we've been taking, web sites we've visited, our emails and tweets, calls we've made, images from closed-circuit (CCTV) security cameras, and a host of other things.

That dispassionate market-based assessment of our identities could even seem to many of us like an invasion of our privacy. In fact, our first question might be, "How did they get all that stuff in the first place? Am I a person, a target, or just a series of data points?" That crunching sound we hear may be someone analyzing our personal data.

Paranoia? *Maybe Not.* **Big Data?** *Maybe.*

In the *face-to-face world*, with the exception of gossip and the grapevine, we have more control over our identity and privacy. In the *online world*, everything seems to be fair game. Invasion of privacy and unwanted attention are commonplace. Say or do something outrageous in the town square or even in your back yard and you may end up with umpteen worldwide hits on YouTube.

Media Literacy. Media literacy skills are becoming essential, since we are often faced with finding the truth among concocted identities designed to influence public opinion. Fabrications spread in an instant by all forms of 24/7 omnipresent media. Each of us needs to be able to separate truth from fiction, which occasionally masquerades as news. Without an understanding of trial by evidence, trial by innuendo might easily triumph.

Losing Control. Growing numbers of people are concerned that our Facebooking, tweeting, and emailing are dashing our ability and willingness to communicate face-to-face. Psychologist Sherry Turkle calls the condition…being *alone together*.[46]

In an article titled, "Silicon Valley Says, 'Step Away from the Device,'" Matt Richtel writes in the *New York Times* that "the lure of constant stimulation—the pervasive demand for pings, rings, and updates—is creating a profound physical craving that can hurt productivity and personal attention."[47]

Identities, Privacy, and Access. Speaking of technology—Given the choice of *privacy* vs. *access to emerging interactive technologies*, there's no contest. Few would disagree that technology, and the avalanche of new apps, has generally won hands-down. One result: nearly anyone can turn a short clip of our lives into a YouTube sensation overnight, for all the world to see.

"Hacktivist" seems to be a growing profession. So are multiple forms of *eavesdropping*, such as the recording of phone calls. Some *identity thieves* prey especially on the young, the elderly, and the ill, knowing they might be vulnerable. *Closed circuit television (CCTV) cameras* seem to be everywhere. *Data mining* can be a double-edged sword. *Wikileaks* and other clandestine hacking and release of information by *insiders* and *outsiders* has put "state secrets" in full view, giving us a window on events and de-

cisions—but sometimes placing people who work in covert activities, perhaps all of us, at risk. You be the judge.

> **"If you are doing something that you would not want a crowd gathered in the town square to know about, consider whether you should be doing it in the first place."**
> *A Rule of Thumb*

Multi-Layered Identity and Privacy Concerns
The Education System

While concerns about identity and privacy are universal, educators are at the center of a whirlwind as they daily confront and deal with a flurry of knotty concerns. The Internet, for example, can be a conduit for legitimate or wayward sharing of private information, which education systems generally have in abundance.

The challenges don't stop there. Security concerns can lead to the use of metal detectors, surveillance cameras, and biometric devices. Both locker-searches and frisking can be highly controversial, even when those who do the searching feel they have "reasonable suspicion" or "probable cause."

• **Family Educational Rights and Privacy Act (FERPA).** This federal law is intended to "protect the privacy of student education records" and "applies to all schools that receive funds under an applicable program of the U.S. Department of Education," according to *ED.gov*.[48]

• **FOIA (Freedom of Information Act).** "The Freedom of Information Act (FOIA) is a law that gives you the right to access information from the federal government. It is often described as the law that keeps citizens in the know about their government."[49] States also have specific "open meeting" or "sunshine laws."

Identity and Privacy...On the Ground
Definitions, Laws, and Challenges

Benefits and consequences of identity and privacy have been magnified. News travels faster than ever. Concerns have become massive.

Social Media. Social media, such as Facebook, Twitter, Instagram, Snapchat, texting, Myspace, Pinterest, Ning, YouTube, Second Life, Reddit, and a host of others, have led to multi-millions of online worldwide connections. We've done friending, photo and video sharing, networking, and co-creating. We've also experienced the intended or unintended benefits and consequences of indiscriminately sharing personal information. While social media can help us build connections with classrooms in other parts of the world, lead us to valuable resources that can enhance education, and create virtual book clubs, they should nonetheless be used safely.[50] Futures Council 21 member Allison LaFave observes that some sites make it possible for people to shape "a digital perception of themselves," making it "difficult to distinguish true reality from perceived reality."

Identity Theft. The U.S. Federal Trade Commission (FTC) has estimated that "as many as nine million Americans have their identities stolen each year." That type of theft takes place when someone "uses your personally identifying information, like your name, Social Security number, or credit card number, without your permission, to commit fraud or other crimes." How do thieves get their hands on our personal information? The Federal Trade Commission (FTC) tells us that they do it by *dumpster diving* (going through your trash), *skimming* (such as stealing credit card information from a device), *phishing* (pretending to gather information for an otherwise legitimate reason), *changing your address and rerouting your mail, old-fashioned stealing*, and *pretexting* (asking you to share information under false pretenses).[51]

Virus protection programs, firewalls, data management firms, encryption, our personal media habits, and shredders are among our first lines of defense.

The Many Faces of Identity

We should do whatever we can to make sure our identity is not co-opted without our knowledge and approval. In schools, for example, some students may find themselves in an "identity group," made up of people with whom they feel they have something in common. More than occasionally, those informal groups can be stereotyped and have their own monikers, such as nerd, geek, bookworm, pot head, loner, clown, gamer, etc.

"**I have preserved my identity, put its credibility to the test, and defended my dignity. What good this will bring the world I don't know. But for me it is good.**"
Vaclav Haval

Implications for Education and Society—*Identity and Privacy*

Implications of identity and privacy for education and the community are so deeply interconnected that they are presented here as one set of possibilities for consideration and further discussion.

• **Getting and Staying Connected.** Concerns about identity and privacy should be addressed with policies, procedures, media literacy education, and personal behavior. Those concerns should not be addressed by becoming disconnected from the wealth of online services and connections that are readily available. Becoming disconnected is a ticket to becoming out-of-touch.

• **Building Understanding of Identity and Privacy.** While virtually everyone is impacted by identity and privacy issues, vast numbers of us need to develop a greater understanding of their magnitude, how they impact us today, and how they could affect our future. Teachers will likely want to make these issues a part of classroom discussions.

• **Stimulating Students to Think about Their Identity and Legacy.** These issues should always be on the agenda. We might want to offer a seminar or finishing school class to help students think deeply about identity and legacy. *One*, they might consider the identity they would prefer versus the identity they are presenting through social networking sites or their personal behavior. *Two*, we could ask students to consider the personal legacy they would like to leave for future generations.

• **Preventing and Dealing with Online Challenges.** As part of personal and technological literacy, students need to fully understand possible dos and don'ts in maneuvering the online world. They might discuss what constitutes appropriate sharing of personal information. These discussions can stimulate dialog across disciplines.

- **Expecting the Inevitable.** Realistically, most organizations, despite their protections, can expect to have their data and information systems invaded by clever and inventive hackers. Despite the immediate problems these types of incidents might cause, they will be even worse if redundancy is not a part of the protection system.

Trend 6: The Economy.
Get Ready for a Reset!

Trend: An economy for a new era will demand restoration and reinvention of physical, social, technological, educational, and policy infrastructure.

> **"The economic crisis doesn't represent a cycle.
> It represents a reset.
> It's an emotional, social, and economic reset."**
> *Jeff Immelt, CEO, General Electric, 2008*[52]

Building on a Firm Foundation
The Future Isn't What It Used to Be!

We are moving from an Industrial Age into a Global Knowledge/ Information Age, accelerating at a rate that could give us whiplash. With barely a stretch, it is also clear that we are headed into an age of knowledge creation and breakthrough thinking.

That's the good news. The glitch is that our infrastructure was created to help us build an economy for yesterday, not for today and tomorrow. Much of that infrastructure is aging, breaking down, or isn't compatible with a flood of new economic realities. It's a dilemma—like trying to squeeze a size 12 foot into a size 8 shoe. Unless we get the right fit for a 21st century economy, we'll be missing opportunities and unable to deal with problems that are growing exponentially.

Infrastructure in Tough Shape. In 2009, the respected American Society of Civil Engineers (ASCE) released a "Report Card on American Infrastructure." By its nature, ASCE focuses primarily on the *built environment*, its resilience and its capacity to serve the systems that depend on it. This particular study zeroed in primarily on the *condition of physical infrastructure*,[53] and helps us see a stark reality even more clearly—we are trying to build a new economy on an often outdated, sometimes crumbling foundation.

Expanding the Concept of Social Infrastructure. Now, let's broaden the concept to encompass a few more essentials in our quest to create a viable infrastructure for the future. Some, but not all, of these items put pressure on us to pave the way for development of our social and intellectual capital. Parts of our social infrastructure might include: a sustainable environment; telecommunication; computer speed and capacity, including download speed; education that is both broad and deep; an ability to tap human imagination, creativity, and ingenuity; innovation and entrepreneurship; and economic, financial, and environmental literacy. All will help move us from an Industrial Age mentality toward 21st century realities.

What Comes First?
How Does the Economy Fit into The Puzzle?

Should civil society and the environment exist simply to serve needs of the economy? or Should socially responsible economic institutions understand that their very existence and success depend on the overall well-being of the world around them? Most thoughtful observers would agree that a legitimate, sustainable, and just economy is a product of a flourishing civil society and a sound environment, coupled with an ongoing investment in the breadth and depth of education.

Big Turnaround and Historic Transitions
We've Been Here Before

Call it a big déjà vu moment for humanity. We're in the midst of another massive social and economic transition. It's one of those great historic shifts whose magnitude might be compared to the move from a hunter-gatherer to an Agricultural Age…then from an Agricultural to an Industrial Age.

These humungous transitions don't happen in a moment. They emerge gradually over generations. If we don't make constant adjustments to our social, economic, and physical infrastructure, we are headed directly toward a brink, a cliff, a crisis, maybe even a catastrophe, whatever term we might choose. One thing we know for sure: even though these transitions have happened throughout history, they can be disorienting, to say the least. These massive resets take place when old systems and infrastructure break down because they are mismatched with new realities.

Challenges and Choices. By 2008, we had moved into a new era, but status quo thinking, a frequent lack of foresight, a shortage of political will, and powerful self-interests whose economic fortunes or personal advantages seemed to be tied to holding up progress, led us to the brink. The Great Recession left us with at least two choices:

• *One,* we could freeze our social and economic infrastructure, let it decay, squeeze out every last drop of profit before it becomes obsolete or illegal, and fight off change.

• *Two,* we could wake up to the need for a renewed infrastructure, ranging from a smart grid and world-class download speeds to education that taps our greatest resource—human ingenuity.

Turbulent, disruptive times can provide an opportunity for each and every one of us to consider where we've been and what we want to strive to become in the future.

The Economy and Education

Schools and colleges have long been seen as the crucible for solving multiple problems or making the most of opportunities facing many countries and communities. As we entered the 21st century, educators had to deal with a mass of new technologies. Yet, some public officials seemed intent on codifying a limited menu of Industrial Age skills and imposing narrow standards and high-stakes tests. Valuable areas of study sometimes dropped from the curriculum since they didn't appear on the required exams.

The Great Recession that began in 2007-08 amplified the need to prepare students for a Global Knowledge/Information Age economy and civil society. At the same time the education system was dealing with the fallout, such as declining tax bases, layoffs, a rise in social problems, and inequities. New demands were landing at their doorsteps. It was a fact that interactive technologies and changes in the trajectory of society demanded education that included a range of 21st century knowledge, skills, behaviors, and attitudes.

Basics of the Industrial Age were still important, but so were creativity, as well as thinking and reasoning, problem solving, and entrepreneurial skills, plus an understanding of the needs of civil society and ethical behavior.

Intellectually and instinctively, people know that education is the foundation for progress. Every institution in society was undergoing massive change, and schools and colleges could not be an exception, since they are *of this world, not separate from it.*

Economic Literacy…Our Futures Are At Stake

Some people get into personal financial hot water, and some organizations, including countries, get into a bind, often because they don't know much about economics or personal finance. Along with civic literacy, economic literacy should be essential.

Concern has grown about people who seem trapped by limited understanding of profit and loss, differences between investments and expenses, needs vs. wants, and a host of other issues. Our understanding of the need to invest in our future is often directly related to the level of our investment in education. Of course, it also helps if we can balance a checkbook and deal with credit card debt.

Implications for Education and Society—*Economy*

Focusing on restoration, reinvention, and expansion of infrastructure; moving from Industrial Age mentalities to Information Age realities; and developing 21st century products and services are a few implications for education and society. Here are more.

• **Establishing a clear and firm relationship between education and both our economy and quality of life.** Every road toward a sound economy and a more civil society runs directly through our education system. As we move even more deeply into a Global Knowledge/Information Age, driven by knowledge creation and breakthrough thinking, educators need to be part of every discussion of a community's or a country's future. In fact, educators will be expected to be in touch with forces in society that have implications for the regional, national, and even international economy.

• **Making education part of our essential infrastructure.** We know that physical infrastructure, such as roads and bridges, must be maintained and repaired. However, we also need to invest in social infrastructure, including education, health, science, research and development, and leadership. Our short- and longer-term economic future depends on producing and encouraging a well-educated workforce.

- **Getting students ready for a new economy.** Economic realities are pulling education needs into clearer focus. First, simply being connected to a plethora of social media and having access to a world of information is not an endpoint in itself. Even though we are moving beyond the Industrial Age, we still need to be industrious and put what we know to work in the economy and civil society. Those who are *not* prepared for a new economy could be among "the new disadvantaged."

- **Insisting that students and others in the community and country are economically and financially literate.** Just as many countries invest too little in civic literacy, they also pay too little attention to economic literacy. Starting at an early age, everyone should be prepared to make rational decisions about needs vs. wants and grasp the idea of dealing with profit and loss, and borrowing and loaning money.

- **Ensuring that preparation and professional development programs challenge habits and mindsets.** That means we'll need to make sure that those on the front lines are prepared through our preparation and professional development programs to keep us on the cutting edge and in sight of the big picture.

Trend 7. Jobs and Careers.
Any openings?

Trend: Pressure will grow for society to prepare
people for jobs and careers that may not
currently exist.

> "It's a recession when your neighbor loses his job;
> it's a depression when you lose yours."
> *Harry S. Truman, Former U.S. President*

Do you have any openings?
I'm looking for a career, but I'll settle for a job.

The race is on. Across the developed and developing world, communities and countries are trying to put people to work. Unemployment and underemployment, wherever they exist, can increase instability, not only in our homes but also in our communities and nations. At its very heart, a strong and stable economy depends on the opportunity for people to work—to find suitable jobs.

Moving from an Industrial Age to a Global Knowledge/Information Age has thrown everyone for a loop. Globalization has led to outsourcing and offshoring. Traditional manufacturing jobs have a way of shifting from one part of the world to another. Streamlined production, automation, and technology have put a crimp in the number of people needed to get some things done. Additive manufacturing, such as 3D printing, could decentralize manufacturing to devices in our own homes. The demand for quarterly profits has trumped loyalty to seasoned employees. In a fast-changing world, new generations of products, even processes, tend to knock old standbys off the shelf.

Creating New Industries and Jobs. Reality is setting in. We will probably not be able to ride our way into the future. We'll have to invent our way into the future. That means every person, community, country, and economy can never stop developing new industries, new careers, and new jobs. It also means that we'll have to constantly create new generations of ideas, technologies, and processes that will turn out an array of products and services capable of measuring up to 21ˢᵗ century expectations. Think of the opportunity: We'll be able to jump start whole new industries that will employ people and create value, whether it's in the for-profit or nonprofit sector. Sadly, some existing industries and clusters of jobs may not make the cut. Thomas Frey, jobs editor for *The Futurist Magazine*, published by the World Future Society, raises another flag. He tells us, "As a rule of thumb, *60 percent of jobs 10 years from now haven't been created yet.*"[54]

Moving Toward Brain-Gain Communities. Unemployment that came with the Great Recession proved to be a stickler for numerous freshly-minted college graduates searching for jobs. Yet, the *education dividend* held fairly firm. For example, in the third-quarter of 2012, people over 25 in the U.S. who were high school graduates, on average, made approximately $9,500 more per year than those without that diploma, according to the Bureau of Labor Statistics (BLS). People with a Bachelor's degree or higher, again on average, made between $42,700 to $155,000 a year *more* than the person without a high school diploma.[55]

It is a fact that education and training generally pay lifetime dividends for people in every demographic group, even though equity remains a continuing challenge. Equal opportunity is essential across all diversities.

"Creatives," who work with a spirit of imagination, invention, innovation, and entrepreneurship, earn more, generally pay more in taxes, support cultural institutions, and build overall economies, author and economic development expert Richard Florida adds.[56] The intensifying demand for knowledge workers poses a growing challenge for the education system and society at large. If a community or country doesn't produce jobs for knowledge workers, then its people will likely migrate and look for other places on the globe where they can profit from their hard work and/or creative genius.

Imagination, creativity, invention, and innovation are keys to moving the economy forward and creating jobs of the future.

Shifts in Employment by Economic Sector. As the focus of our local and national economies has shifted, we've had to deal with a scourge of unemployment and underemployment. It's not what we'd like, but it's a reality we need to address squarely.

The Bureau of Labor Statistics (BLS) keeps a tab on employment in major sectors of the economy. The three that get primary attention are agriculture, industry, and services. Take a look at trend lines reflected in the figure below.

In his book, *The Great Reset*, Richard Florida argues that the time has come to turn growing numbers of service jobs into really good ones that pay decently and provide learning and growth opportunities. It's a value-add for any organization and boosts esprit-de-corps.[57]

Shares of Economic Sectors in the Labor Force (Percent)

Economic Sector	1840	1900	1950	2000	2010	2020
Agricultural	69	37	12	1.6	1.5	1.2
Industrial	15	30	35	16.8	12.4	11.9
Services	17	33	53	73.8	78.8	79.9
Other Combinations	N.A.	N.A.	N.A.	7.8	7.4	6.9
Total	101	100	100	100	100.1	99.9

Percentages for 1840 through 1950 drawn from Historical Statistics of the United States, Bureau of the Census, 1960[58]. Those for 2000 and 2010 plus projections for 2020 drawn from "Employment by Major Industry Sector," U.S. Bureau of Labor Statistics.[59] "Other Combinations" includes secondary agriculture, private household, family worker, or self-employed. Details may not total 100 percent due to rounding.

Outsourcing and Insourcing

Some organizations employ people who are not on staff to perform certain functions, occasionally in the hope of saving money and often because the firm has certain work to do but not enough of it to justify hiring someone full-time. That's generally called *outsourcing*. Sometimes, it all happens locally. When that work is done in another country, we often refer to it as offshoring. Occasionally, people call it, "shipping jobs overseas." Observers believe an inshoring trend might be developing, driven by higher-priced shipping fuel, new technologies, and higher productivity.

Fastest Growing and Fastest Declining Occupations[60]

The U.S. Bureau of Labor Statistics (BLS) forecasts both fastest growing and fastest declining occupations. On the plus side, the personal health care aides occupation will likely experience 70 percent growth between 2010 and 2020; home health aides, 69 percent growth; registered nurses, 26 percent; receptionists and information clerks, 24 percent; and elementary and postsecondary teachers, 17 percent. Fastest declining occupations include: shoe machine operators and tenders, some Postal Service positions, fabric and apparel patternmakers, and switchboard operators. [61]

Futurist David Pearce Snyder sees "a huge opportunity and need for reskilling/upskilling over 40 million adults in the U.S., including, in 2013, 24+ million un- or under-employed workers."

Welcome to the Home Office.

You're right, home office has taken on another meaning. On the one hand, it could be the headquarters of the company. On another, it could just be an office in your home that you use to telecommute. Writing for *Associations Now*, Katie Bascuas observed that, "While opponents of teleworking argue that working outside the office can reduce collaboration, innovation, and productivity, proponents point to business benefits such as reduced operational or real estate costs, improved continuity of service, and reduced absenteeism."[62]

Hot Prospects for the Future
New Wrinkles

"One of the easiest ways to begin thinking about future careers is to focus on what may be a problem in the future and invent a job that solves it," suggests Cynthia Wagner, editor of the World Future Society's *Futurist Magazine*.[63]

Try this. We can divine possible jobs for the future by studying each or combinations of the trends included in this book, then asking, "What kind of jobs will we need to create to deal with it?"

Try these obvious job possibilities, again drawn from various chapters of *Twenty-One Trends*: data analytics; neuroscience; superconducting technologist or electro-chemist; energy innovator, entrepreneur, and technician; robotics engineer, inventor, technician, and ethicist; and nano-, bio-, and forensic scientist and technologist.

So What Are *Employability Skills?*

Even if we're self-employed, having certain employability skills will likely improve our shot at success. The classic and rather timeless *SCANS Report*, issued in 1991 by the U.S. Department of Labor, is consistent with employability skills that were still being sought more than 20 years later. They include:

• **Basic Skills:** reading, writing, arithmetic, mathematics, listening, and speaking.

• **Thinking Skills:** creative thinking, decision-making, problem solving, visualization, knows/learns, reasoning.

• **Personal Qualities:** responsibility, self-worth, sociability, self-management, and integrity/honesty.

• **Work Competencies:** utilizing resources, interpersonal skills, utilizing information, using systems, and using technology.[64]

In an article titled, "What You Don't Know Will Hurt You," written by contributor Kathy Caprino, *Forbes* listed eight essential skills for professionals. Among them: communication, building relationships, decision-making, leadership, the ability to advocate and negotiate for yourself and your causes, planning and management, having a sense of work-life balance, and boundary enforcement (knowing yourself, your needs and wants, and what, for you, is non-negotiable).[65]

The Conference Board of Canada, in its *Employability Skills 2000+*, emphasizes fundamental, personal management, and teamwork skills.[66] Clearly, collaboration is fast becoming central to employability.

College of Arts & Sciences Dean Matthew Moen raises a caution for policymakers who "continue to drive universities to become engines of economic development rather than repositories of wisdom." Ed Gordon, president of Imperial Consulting in Chicago, a noted workforce development expert and author of *Future Jobs*, reinforces the need for a foundation in the liberal arts and an education-talent creation system.[67]

Career Education
What am I gonna do?

While all education, including life experiences, might be considered preparation for a career, sorting out the multitude of possibilities and matching them to our talents, abilities, and interests can be tough. That's why career education is vitally important.

Most agree on some grouping of knowledge, skills, and behaviors that are basic to career education. Examples include: career awareness and preparation, attitude development, career exploration, internships, career acquisition (getting a job), career retention (keeping a job), advancement, and entrepreneurship.[68]

Implications for Education and Society—*Jobs and Careers*

• **Education systems at all levels will face growing demand to produce good members of civil society who are employable and prepared for jobs and careers in a 21st century global economy.** Educators and community leaders will face demands from both the public and private sectors to produce people who are "college and career ready." Every student, every potential worker, will require the breadth and depth of education and the flexibility to become a contributing member of civil society and a fast-changing national and world economy.

• **Communities and countries will need to become and remain competitive for talent and resources.** We may want to grow our local or national economies, but we will always be faced with some tough questions. *One*, "Is this a place I'd want to live?" *Two*, "Can I make enough money to sustain myself and my family?" Whether we like it or not, egos aside, we're in competition for both talent and resources.

• **Fresh approaches will be needed to teach career and entrepreneurial skills.** Career and vocational education will constantly take on a greater dynamic as it responds to realities and possibilities in both the for-profit and not-for-profit world. In addition to being employable, potential workers will generally need entrepreneurial skills to succeed, whether in an existing job or career or one they invent.

• **Educators will be among those who are deeply involved in discussions about economic development and quality of life in ev-**

ery community. That, of course, means that educators will stay in constant touch with the world outside the trenches. Constantly scanning the environment and anticipating possibilities for social and economic development is baseline. Demand will grow for people with the education and training to perform as members of an international/global economy. The status quo is unsustainable.

• **Education and training programs and systems will need to reflect changes in industries and careers—and be able and willing to adapt.** Careers that capture the interest of students might change frequently in response to the job market and employment opportunities. As part of that responsiveness, schools and colleges will continue to be centers for continuing education, training and retraining, elder care, and other services, possibly all under one roof.

Trend 8: Energy. *It's a Power Game.*

Trend: The need to develop new sources of affordable and accessible energy will lead to intensified scientific invention and political tension.

|| **"Energy is the life blood of advanced civilizations."**
|| *World Changing, Edited by Alex Steffen*[69]

Energy: One Thing We All Have in Common.

Just to be clear, one of the greatest sources of energy is the ingenuity of people. In fact, that creative energy is essential if we hope to meet the challenge of powering our economy and our civil society as we move toward a more sustainable future. If there is one thing we all have in common, it is our need for energy.

Constant, clean, reliable sources of energy are basic to our existence. Our economy and civil society are, to say the least, *energy-dependent*. Some even tell us that we're *addicted to oil*—that we've become *energy junkies*.

Where Do We Get Our Energy?

Backing off to the big picture, there are basically two types of energy: *nonrenewable* and *renewable*, which could also be described as *finite* and *infinite*. According to a U.S. Department of Energy Education and Workforce Development presentation, *nonrenewables* will "eventually dwindle, becoming too expensive or too environmentally damaging to retrieve." *Renewables* or infinite sources "do not use up natural resources or harm the environment and can be replaced in a short period of time."

Of course, the times demand increased investment in *research and development (R&D)*, and that must be coupled with *political will* and *a sense of urgency*, if we hope to dig out of our energy trenches.

Nonrenewables. Sources of energy that might, over time, be depleted are fossil fuels that resulted from "the remains of plants and other organisms buried in the earth's crust and altered by heat and pressure over millions of years." While generally thriving, existing extraction industries understand the need to develop an even more extensive energy mix. Among those sources are coal, petroleum, natural gas, and uranium.

Renewables. Sources of energy generally described as *renewables*, sometimes as *clean energy* or *alternatives*, include solar, wind, hydrogen, hydroelectric (water), geothermal, and biomass.[70] The scientists, technicians, and a host of others who pursue these sources might be called *energy harvesters*.

Getting increased attention are *space-based solar collectors* that might orbit the planet; *lunar-based solar collectors*; *heat vacuums* to capture heat from asphalt roads and parking lots; and *embedded pvcs* in roofing and other building materials plus other public spaces, including roads.

Energy Production and Consumption…by the Numbers

While some people rave, accuse, and occasionally bend numbers to make a case for their special interest, whatever it might be, here are a few basic facts about energy production and consumption from the U.S. Energy Information Administration (EIA) and other sources.

In 2011, domestic energy production met about 80 percent of U.S. energy demand. That meant, as the second decade of the 21st century got under way, the country was relying on imports for approximately 20 percent of energy needs. That reality has introduced issues such as *energy dependence*, reaching *energy independence*, or pursuing *energy interdependence*.

In 2012, petroleum led the way in energy consumption at 36 percent, followed by natural gas at 25 percent, and coal at 20 percent.[71] Primary uses of energy in school buildings included space heating and cooling, water heating, and lighting.[72]

Personal and Public Transportation

Driven by inevitably higher energy costs and the environmental impact of CO_2 and other emissions, consumers are looking for more efficient trains, planes, automobiles, and other vehicles. Aircraft manufacturers, for example, have made fuel efficiency a major target. Auto manufacturers have been turning out more hybrid and electric cars. Railroads tout their tons of freight hauled per unit of energy burned.

The Energy Infrastructure
A Look at Transmission/Distribution, Efficiency, and Storage

From the beginning, even as Thomas Edison built his first system for generating electricity, he had to deal with distribution of that power to those who needed and wanted it. The expanding enterprise became a model for *systemic innovation.*

Years later, the energy infrastructure, in many parts of the world, simply must be updated to meet the needs of an emerging high-tech economy and growing demand from civil society. That includes the need for energy efficiency and reliability.

Smart Grid. Improving and in some cases replacing a big slice of our energy infrastructure by moving to a *smart grid* is no small matter. Replacing 215,000 miles of high-voltage power lines in the U.S. could cost an estimated $1.5 trillion over 20 years, according to *The Daily Beast.*

Benefits of a smart grid might include: "more efficient transmission, quicker restoration of electricity if it goes down, reduced operating costs, reduced peak demand, increased integration of large-scale renewable energy systems, and better integration of customer-owned power generation systems, including renewable energy."[73] In short, you will likely be able to sell any power you generate and don't use back to the grid.

Energy Storage. The demand for smaller, more powerful, longer-lasting batteries seems to grow exponentially in direct proportion to the number of smartphones we're carrying or hybrid, all-electric, or solar-powered cars we're driving.

Relentless research and development are under way to develop advanced batteries. In many cases, that means "grid-scale," "utility-scale" storage. That would allow for, among other things, "transmission and distribution deferral," smoothing out the power supply as it is needed on the grid.

Think about industries, jobs, and careers. Electrochemists, superconducting technologists, and people involved in photonics, among others, will be working to increase battery power and further develop the smart grid.[74]

Energy Literacy

Energy is important to our quality of life, even our existence. That's reason enough for all of us to be energy literate. We're not necessarily talking about another course in school. However, we are being challenged to address this big question: *What do all of us need to know about energy?* The U.S. Department of Energy, working with the American Association for the Advancement of Science (AAAS) and numerous other organizations, has developed a booklet, available online, titled *Energy Literacy…Essential Principles and Fundamental Concepts for Energy Education.*[75]

Implications for Education and Society—*Energy*

• **Be ready for changes in lifestyles.** Some will want to live nearer work to reduce transportation costs and help address environmental concerns. Demand will grow for expansion of mass transit.

• **Expect demand for energy education.** Energy literacy will become a significant aim for every student and educator. Worldwide, people will expect schools and colleges to help students understand and be able to address energy challenges.

• **Consider new energy-related industries and their job-creating potential.** Every challenge brings an opportunity. Renewable energy will become a growth industry and a source of jobs and careers.

• **Insist that current sources of energy are efficient, broadly available, and people-friendly.** To ensure quality of life, each person must have access to affordable clean energy. Be prepared to address the tension between short-term profits and long-term health, even survival, issues that have become more acute across the energy spectrum. Start conversations about the quality of life we might expect moving forward.

- **Promote sustainable energy for your community.** As a community, look beyond the moment. Consider future energy needs. Do short-, medium-, and longer-term plans to provide the energy you'll need in the future.
- **Consider science first; then develop political positions.** Scientific knowledge continues to expand. A massive body of that work has been devoted to studying energy and the environment. To the extent possible, we should try to build our political positions on top of scientific realities.
- **Be ready to consider and support research and development.** Unfortunately, we invest too little in R&D. When legitimate opportunities arise to support it, we should give those proposals our serious consideration. Then, we should strongly consider investments we need to make in improving our energy future.
- **Education systems at every level will have frequently updated plans for energy use and conservation.** In the process of developing and implementing plans, educators might involve members of the community and staff as well as students.
- **Education and other institutions will likely face rising energy costs.** What schools and colleges have to invest in actual instruction could be profoundly impacted by the rising cost of powering electronic technologies, transporting students, keeping lights on, and providing for heating and cooling.
- **Students can practice their thinking and reasoning skills as they consider energy challenges.** Learning about capturing and conserving energy will energize classroom discussions. Teachers will have an opportunity to ask students to use their creativity and imaginations in considering energy concerns and opportunities.

Trend 9: Environmental and Planetary Security. *Where is Paul Revere?*

Trend: Common opportunities and threats will intensify a worldwide demand for planetary security.

> **"We haven't inherited this planet from our parents, we've borrowed it from our children."**
> *Jane Goodall, British Primologist and Anthropologist*[76]

A Balancing Act for Survival

If you're like most of us, you're deeply committed to personal security. Some of us, in fact, are even willing to trade some of our basic freedoms for what we hope will make and keep us safe. Many students of human behavior tell us we're driven by self-interest, certainly by self-preservation. Some organizations fight for their corporate interest. What can override all of these interests and yearnings for safety and security? The answer is *planetary security.* Everything around us exists in the environment. Destroy that…and all bets are off.

During 2012, scientists issued a sort of report card. Scientific instruments detected that carbon dioxide levels in the atmosphere had reached 400 parts per million, a level not seen on earth for three million years, long before the roughly 8,000 years that relatively civilized humans have occupied the planet.[77]

Let's face it, it will be the students in our schools and colleges today who will develop the ideas, techniques, technologies, behaviors, and lifestyles that will help us sustain this planet. Unless they have some understanding of the issues they confront, they may have a tough time dealing with them…or even grasping the growing sense of urgency. They may be missing one or several fundamentals for our very survival.

Who will call on us to take action? Where is the next Paul Revere?

A Growing Sense of Urgency
Climate Change

A *National Geographic* documentary, *About Six Degrees Could Change the World*, attempted to explain the impact of climate change on temperatures. Author, journalist, and environmentalist Mark Lynas, who wrote *Six Degrees*, followed scientists who explained what to expect with various increases in the average world temperature.

• We're on track for a .5 to 1 degree C (0.9 to 1.8 F) increase in temperature. We've seen extreme weather and melting ice in glaciers and polar regions.

• A 2 C (3.6 degrees F) increase would lead to the disappearance of glaciers and some lower lying islands.

• "At 3 degrees C (5.4 degrees F) higher, the Arctic would be ice free all summer; the Amazon rainforests would begin to dry out; and extreme weather patterns would become the norm." [78]

An unavoidable conclusion is that our personal security depends on the security of our planet. We are past the point that any one group, wherever it is, can survive only at the expense of others.

How will we be remembered?

In *The Third Industrial Revolution*, economist and author Jeremy Rifkin asks us to think about what our age might be called, if humanity survives. He speculates that we might be called "the fossil fuel people and the period (might be referred to) as the Carbon Era, just as we have referred to past periods as the Bronze and Iron Ages."[79]

Common Threats and Common Opportunities
Natural and Human Caused Environmental Threats

Nothing galvanizes us more than common threats or common opportunities. Unfortunately, it has too often taken natural or human-caused disasters to rally our attention. Opportunities never seem as compelling as threats.

Perhaps that is why we are constantly threatened—because we fail to recognize and pursue the opportunities that surround us. Damage control has become the new norm, but will there come a time when we ultimately do damage that is beyond repair?

Natural Threats. Massive changes in the ecology of our planet have likely been caused by events of nature, such as volcanic activity, earthquakes, or direct hits by meteorites, asteroids, or comets, according to scientific consensus.

Other natural disasters, such as those caused by floods, hurricanes, typhoons, droughts, heat waves and extreme cold, snowstorms and blizzards, desertification, tsunamis, and possible asteroid or meterorite strikes have largely been thought to be somewhat predictable, minimally controllable, and largely unpreventable. All can cause death, injuries, displacement of people, and heavy economic and social consequences, as we've witnessed time and again.

Human-Caused Threats. Instability can lead to threats, which often have worldwide implications. Just a few of those threats include terrorism; extreme income disparities among and within nations; genocide and the massive number of refugees, many displaced by environmental factors; steadily increasing carbon emissions that trap heat in the atmosphere and raise global temperatures; poverty and armed conflict; and both natural and human resources that are being commandeered to support the drug trade, combat, and suppression. "As much as 24 percent of global disease is caused by environmental exposures which can be averted," according to the World Health Organization (WHO).

Common Opportunities. One thing we know with some certainty. The earth's species have been adapting to life on this planet for millions of years. We do not have evidence of a nearby planet that could readily sustain us. In short, we have nowhere else to go. That should be incentive enough to see problems as opportunities in disguise.

To the extent we've been trying to ignore environmental problems, that cost of neglect has passed its due date. We are surrounded by both problems and opportunities. Think, for example, about employment opportunities that could be created by seriously pursuing any or all of these possibilities:

- Harvesting renewable sources of energy and increasing battery capacity.

- Conceiving of treatments, cures, and prevention strategies for diseases.
- Creating technologies and treaties that will guarantee adequate fresh water.
- Promoting and supporting even better environmental education.

"Man shapes himself through decisions that shape his environment."
Rene Dubos, French-American Microbiologist

Implications for Education and Society— *Personal/Planetary Security*

The following implications have repercussions for both education and the whole of society as we work together to address our individual and planetary security.

- **Balancing economic development and environmental sustainability.** As we make progress in our communities, in our nation, and globally, we need to measure what we do against its impact on our environment and our legacy for future generations.

- **Insisting on environmental education.** The evidence is multiplying that our environment is in peril, and so are all of us who occupy the planet. To solve these problems, we must overcome the gridlock as we make the case for a sense of urgency. Environmental education in our schools and communities is one important step.

Tokyo International School Vision Navigator Patrick Newell raises a compelling concern: "The time has come to reconnect with nature. A survey recently found that 16 to 22-year-olds preferred having a connection with digital tools over smell."

- **Making study of the environment an interdisciplinary springboard for creativity, problem solving, media literacy, an understanding of globalization, and other areas of study.** This multidisciplinary concern can be addressed in courses or units in science, math, engineering, technology, business, economics, social sciences, civic education, law-related education, international education, government, media literacy, communication, and environmental studies, to name a few.

• **Creating environmentally friendly schools and other buildings.** Buildings provide an "envelope" where people generally gather to work or learn, often both. They are also symbols for how we think and feel about the environment.

• **Offering futures courses.** As students study futures, they develop techniques for better understanding the social, political, economic, technological, demographic, and environmental forces that drive us today and shape tomorrow.

Trend 10: Sustainability. *Bearable, Viable, and Equitable*

Trend: Sustainability will depend on adaptability and resilience in a fast-changing, at-risk world.

> **"What's the use of a fine house if you haven't got a tolerable planet to put it on?"**
> *Henry David Thoreau[80]*

Great Idea! But is it Sustainable?

That's a question that pops up virtually everywhere. Generally understood as the *ability to endure*, sustainability has become a flagship concern for the environment and the economy. While its implications are spread across those and other chapters of this book, the urgency of sustainability is ingrained in every problem we solve and every issue we address in nearly every walk of life. That's why we're briefly setting it apart and putting it in the spotlight.

Sustainability is another elephant in the room, so big that we sometimes don't even see it. In fact, in a polarized society, where honest discussion becomes buried in political rhetoric, that herd of elephants in the room seems to be increasing exponentially.

Sustainable: (a). relating to, or being a method of harvesting or using a resource so that the resource is not depleted or permanently damaged. (b). of or relating to a lifestyle involving the use of sustainable methods. *Synonyms:* defendable, defensible, justifiable, maintainable, supportable, tenable. *Antonyms:* indefensible, insupportable, unjustifiable, unsustainable, untenable. *Merriam-Webster Dictionary Online.*[81] Additional definitions include the ability to endure, prolong, keep up, exist, and to nourish.

Sustainability
Back to Basics

Let's start with the environment and call it our *natural capital*. If the environment provides the ingredients for life, we'll be able to exist and possibly even become self-sustaining. At some point, we might develop a society that thrives because of the contributions of *human capital*. Based on the foundation of natural and human capital, various forms of industry might develop. We'll call that *economic capital*. As simple as it seems, the whole thing is truly profound. Fundamentally, the environment and society don't exist because of the economy, but the economy exists on a foundation of natural and human capital.

Of course, social, environmental, and economic spheres overlap. At the intersections of those forces, we have an opportunity to think about whether our dreams and plans will be *bearable*, *viable*, and *equitable*.[82] If what we're considering doesn't pass the test, it may simply not be sustainable.

Nature. The Industrial Revolution left the impression that we could do whatever we pleased with our natural environment and it wouldn't fight back. If we continue to consume as we have been, we'll likely need four or five planets to sustain us. While we might follow the environmental arguments of our favorite political commentators, nature keeps right on following the laws of science.

Implications for Education and Society—*Sustainability*

• Leaders should expect to be constantly challenged with maintaining the sustainability of their schools or colleges and the future of their communities.

• Demand will grow for more sustainable buildings and an infrastructure that is not only built to endure but also subject to ongoing maintenance and repair.

• Sustainability should be part of the discussion whenever we consider world, national, community, and personal decisions.

• Units, courses, and degree programs in sustainability are likely to increase at schools and colleges in response to growing demand and the urgency of societal need.

- In areas of the curriculum such as economics, social studies, environmental studies, technology, mathematics, physical and biological sciences, and other subjects, students will be expected to learn how they can apply the principles of sustainability.

- In the hands of creative educators, students, and others in the community, discussions of this concept can help build a more sustainable future for our education system, economy, and civil society.

Trend 11: International/Global.
We're all in this together.

Trend: International learning, including relationships, cultural understanding, languages, and
diplomatic skills, will become basic.

Sub-trend: To earn respect in an interdependent
world, nations will be expected to demonstrate
their reliability and tolerance.

Did you know?

The facts are stunning. According to the U.N. Population Division, for
every 100 people who live on the planet, 60 percent live in Asia, 15 percent in Africa, 11 percent in Europe, 9 percent in Latin America and the
Caribbean, 1 percent in Oceania, and 5 percent in Northern America.[83]

The World
How Small Is It?

The earth has somehow gotten smaller. If Greece catches a cold,
people in other parts of the world start to sneeze. If a nuclear reactor
goes off kilter in Asia, nations an ocean away start testing for radia-
tion. Even though the road has not been smooth, we are moving from
isolationist independence toward a realization that the people of this
relatively small blue planet are interdependent.

How Flat is It?

The World is Flat. That's the title of *New York Times* columnist and
author Thomas Friedman's now classic book, first published in 2005.
So what is he getting at? While you can read the book and draw your
own conclusions, most of us likely agree on a few basics. *One,* the playing field is being leveled. *Two,* a long list of technologies, including
many that will continue to emerge, make it possible for people to work,

in essence, side-by-side, even if they are physically thousands of miles away.[84] It's a convergence, a connectedness, and a part of the foundation for an increasingly global society.

A 2012 Harvard Future of Learning Institute defined globalization as "the accelerating traffic of people, capital, and cultural products around the world. (It) embodies opportunities and risks for individuals and societies worldwide."[85]

Globalization...Educators Weigh In

Globalization is happening in real time, and everyone, everywhere, feels its impact, whether they want to admit it or not. There is nowhere to hide, whether we work in government, business, education, or any other field. We've listened to some seasoned educators who shared observations about this phenomenon.

Joseph Hairston, President and CEO of Vision Unlimited in Maryland, foresees "the flat world becoming evident in our schools. Multicultural environments will expand in our classrooms as learning becomes an *anywhere anytime* experience."

Debra Hill, an associate professor at Argosy University in Chicago, a longtime K-12 educator, and a former ASCD president, calls for multiple language acquisition.

James Harvey, executive director of the National Superintendents Roundtable, emphasizes the need for "a new emphasis on developing global competency in our graduates—with more attention in the curriculum to history, geography, and languages."

Joseph Cirasuolo, executive director of the Connecticut Association of Public School Superintendents (CAPSS), makes clear that if we do not "educate all children from a global perspective, they will be ill equipped to be productive in a global economy."

For all leaders, one thing is becoming crystal clear. As we move into the future, getting things done will mean reaching across cultures, habits, histories, ideas, points of view, prejudices, and time zones.

Growth and Shift
As the World Churns

In 1960, the world population neared 3 billion. By 2000, it had doubled to 6 billion and passed 7 billion in 2011. That's right. The population doubled in just 40 years. By 2050, the U.S. Census Bureau is expecting the world population to reach more than 9 billion. That's a 50 percent increase in just 50 years.[86] Consider this. While *less developed or developing countries* were expected to grow by 60 percent, *more developed countries* were projected to grow only 4 percent. The challenge is apparent.

National Reputations...
They depend on each of us and all of us.

Over time, national reputations become directly tied to the level of respect any country enjoys as a member of the community of nations. That level of respect could ultimately be a key to a country's success, even its survival.

Let's take a quick look at some of the most basic of those international relationships. They include relationships among governments; business relationships; educational, scientific, and other non-governmental relationships; and personal relationships. Of course, they range from trade agreements and international help in times of need to exchanges of information, the marketing of products and services, and travel. Most would agree that all are enhanced or inhibited, depending on the situation, by instant electronic communication and a 24/7 news cycle. Every student who emerges from our schools and colleges should understand these critical relationships.

Hot-Button Realities...
For Globally Sensitive Schools, Communities, and Countries

The road to helping students, educators, communities, countries, and continents become more sensitive to international/global issues is getting busier. The traffic is intense because the sense of urgency is increasing exponentially. Thinking is expanding beyond traditional boundaries at the same time the planet seems to be shrinking. With that in mind, here are a few hot-button realities that deserve our attention.

Among those hot button realities is the need to *think globally and act locally*. Another reality is the need to *balance international competition with international cooperation.* A constant challenge for every country is to *balance sovereignty* and *collaboration* in a way that we can become good members of *a family of nations.*

Brain Gain vs. Brain Drain has become a stark reality. Unless we provide opportunities for people to use their talents, abilities, and outright genius in our own communities or countries, they will move on. Some call it *brain circulation.*

Workforce mobility is a driving issue with massive impact on *jobs and careers.* The competition for resources, including human resources, will continue, as it has for centuries, even millennia. If we hope to retain or attract people, we need to be attractive.

Immigration/migration, acceptance, and language are and will remain hot-button realities. All children, whatever their parentage or social and economic circumstances, will need equal access to a broad, deep, and purposeful education. That includes opportunities for them to fill any gaps and get on a level playing field so that they can become contributing members of the economy and civil society. Add to all of that the need to feel accepted. Of course, a basic acceptance of *human rights* will be an assurance that any progress is built on a firm foundation.

International Students and Exchanges. Those who have, perhaps, some of the most in-depth experiences are international students who study or work on projects abroad. In 2010-11, the Institute for International Education (IIE) noted that 273,996 U.S. students were studying abroad. In 2011-12, 764,495 international students were studying in U.S. colleges and universities.

The Massive Growth of Mega-Cities.

"By 2030, the world's urban population alone will have grown to almost 5 billion, with growth centering on cities as rural area populations shrink."[87] In 1970, only two metro areas had become mega-cities or agglomerates of 10 million or more, Tokyo and New York. By *1990*, it was 13; and by *2011*, 23. Projections put the number of mega-cities of 10 million+ at 37 by *2025*, with 21 of those cities in Asia and three in the U.S.

Guideposts for International/Global Education

The ball is squarely in our court. The world is changing before our very eyes. As educators, what are we doing to get our students, our whole societies, in sync with tectonic shifts and quantum leaps into an interconnected future?

Fernando Reimers is the Ford Foundation Professor of International Education, Director of Global Education, and Director of the International Education Policy Program at Harvard. Writing for ASCD's September 2009 issue of *Educational Leadership*, Reimers remarked:

"Good educators know that the real world is ever more interconnected and interdependent. We all (face) planetary challenges such as climate change, health epidemics, global poverty, global economic recessions and trade imbalances, assaults on human rights, terrorism, political instability, international trade, and international cooperation. These challenges and opportunities define the contours of our lives, even in their most local dimensions. Yet in spite of growing awareness of the importance of developing global skills, few students around the world have the opportunity today to become globally competent."[88]

Craig Perrier, a Fairfax County, Virginia, high school social studies specialist, recommends global competency skills, such as: understanding global systems; foreign language acquisition; a grounding in world history, geography, international institutions, and cross-cultural collaboration; and a grasp of concepts such as culture, gender, race, ethnicity, and power.

Diplomatic Qualities and Skills. In a world grown small, countries earn their respect by regularly demonstrating that they are connected to their own citizens and considerate of their neighbors. That simple but stark fact has significant implications for schools and colleges and for international education. For one, it means all students should have at least basic *diplomatic qualities, skills, and knowledge*, such as open minds, natural curiosity, patience, courtesy and good manners, a sense of tolerance, and the ability to empathize with others—to put themselves in someone else's shoes.[89]

International Testing and Assessment. A variety of assessments attempt to provide comparative data on how students are doing from one country to the next. While rankings of participating countries might vary from one testing period to the next, and some question their overall usefulness in improving education, the studies provide a scorecard and observations that can stimulate discussion about a range of education issues in a global context. Among them are PISA, TIMSS, and PIRLS.

> **"The pervasive lack of knowledge about foreign cultures and foreign languages threatens the security of the United States as well as its ability to compete in the global marketplace and produce an informed citizenry."**
> *National Research Council*
> *International Education and Foreign Languages: Keys to Securing America's Future.*[90]

Implications for Education and Society—*Global/International*

• **The urgency of international/global learning will grow exponentially.** The stakes are high and the possible benefits so great that schools and colleges will be expected to strengthen their international and global education programs.

• **Curriculum should include the building blocks for international/global education.** The critical and growing demand for international learning has direct implications for world languages and history, international relations, diplomatic skills, and cultural understanding. *The reality:* Untold numbers of organizations employ and are run by people from around the globe. Today's students will work in and even lead some of those organizations and need to be ready to collaborate with people whose cultures and languages may not match their own.

• **Attracting, growing, and keeping multinational businesses and other institutions will require an environment of acceptance and support.** As communities, regions, and countries build their futures, they might encourage local or regional entrepreneurs to develop multinational businesses or other institutions. Attracting and keeping those types of ventures in our communities will require understanding, acceptance, and support.

• **Students could identify characteristics of any country that hopes to become a respected member of a family of nations.** Have students do brainstorming as they consider a measuring stick or a set of criteria that might apply to any nation, not just their own. Taking the process a step further, students and communities could expand their conversation to consider the impact of those criteria on national or even local futures.

Trend 12: Personalization.
Let's get personal.

Trend: In a world of diverse talents and aspirations, we will increasingly discover and accept that one size does not fit all.

> "Today you are You. That is truer than true.
> There is no one alive who is Youer than You."
> *Dr. Seuss*[91]

Personalizing education isn't new, but it's getting more attention because the stakes for our future are so high. An aim is to provide more options in considering "what is learned, when it is learned, and how it is learned." It is a way to get education even better aligned with a student's individual learning style and multiple intelligences.[92] The U.S. Department of Education defines personalization, at least in part, as "instruction that is paced to learning needs, tailored to learning preferences, and tailored to the specific interests of different learners."[93]

Despite the differences, a one-size model has too often been locked-in by imposing standards and high stakes tests. Educators feel they are forced to dig even deeper, hoping to strike a vein of better test scores on a few subjects.

At the same time, the clamor inside and outside those trenches is getting louder. Legions of people realize that our very future will depend on paying attention to the uniqueness of each learner, along with emphasizing how to work as part of a team.

Educators on Personalization

A National Middle Level Principal of the Year and now a Montana superintendent, *Laurie Barron* is determined to close achievement gaps. She calls for "multiple sources of data for each individual student, including standardized test scores, universal screeners, classroom pre- and post-tests, and other formative assessments, so that teachers can truly customize instruction for each student."

Argosy University Associate Professor and 2012 ASCD President *Debra Hill* calls for a "growth model." She supports "multiple measures to determine where each child actually is on the academic spectrum, rather than assuming that every child ends up in the same place."

The Standards and Testing Conundrum

Let's admit it. Many of us are hooked on a scoreboard mentality. We want *summative* test results, like the score we get at the end of a football game. Perhaps even more important are *formative* tests that can guide us toward more personalized learning and maybe even higher achievement for all students. A note of caution. High-stakes standardized test scores, if they become the end-all goal of education, can potentially freeze the system into a lockstep that overlooks individual differences and the stark reality of a world that will simply not stand still, not for a minute. Few, if any, tests measure a full range of talents and abilities. Much of what we'll need to know and be able to do in the future may not even show up on our radar, because we'll have to incite the curiosity of students to invent it.

As the nation entered the 2010s, Common Core Standards were developed largely by two state-based organizations, the Council of Chief State School Officers (CCSSO) and the National Governors Association (NGA). To begin, internationally benchmarked Common Core standards addressed math and English language arts. The groups went on to explain, "Of course, other subject areas are critical to young people's education and their success in college and careers."[94]

All students, despite their social, economic, or other backgrounds, need to have a chance to succeed. Recognizing and striving to meet the need for personalization is a powerful force for improvement in education, and it could pay huge dividends.

Barron adds that, if an important goal is high achievement, "there should be multiple paths to meet that goal: personalization."

> "Not everything that counts can be counted,
> and not everything that can be counted counts."
> *Albert Einstein*[95]

Five Dimensions of Personalization

Give some thought to these five forces that are fast becoming staples of the personalization mix. With massive migration, **globalization** will help determine the variety of people who land on the doorsteps of our schools and colleges. **Technology** will help us tailor content and instruction for students and make it available anytime, anywhere. The fast-emerging field of **Mind-Brain and Education**[96], a branch of neuroscience, will provide even more discrete information about how students learn. **Scans, pharmaceuticals, and enhancements**, from fMRI scans to performance-enhancing medications and augmented reality, we should look for multiple possibilities.

Another is **Multiple Intelligences.** Personalizing education, moving away from the one-size-fits-all model isn't a fad or necessarily a movement. It is becoming a reality. We know that we are not dealing with cookie-cutter kids. Each one is unique. Round pegs don't fit into square holes, but that doesn't mean we don't need round pegs.

Perhaps the most focused contemporary approaches to personalizing education have been driven by Howard Gardner's classic work, *Frames of Mind*, published in 1983. He expanded on that work in *Multiple Intelligences...The Theory in Practice*, published in 1993. Gardner's premise is that each of us has some mix of seven or more intelligences," which he defines as musical, bodily-kinesthetic, logical-mathematical, linguistic, spatial, interpersonal, and intrapersonal. Gardner's theories are based on cognitive research.[97]

A 2010 Software & Information Industry Association (SIIA), ASCD, and Council of Chief State School Officers (CCSSO) study concluded, in part, that a key element of personalizing education is "flexible, anytime, everywhere learning."[98]

Implications for Education and Society—*Personalization*

• **Constructively answering the call for personalized education.** An expectation for personalization has reached every corner of society and crosses the demographic landscape, from social and economic conditions and racial and ethnic diversity to those who qualify for special education. That demand will not go away.

• **Nurturing a climate that includes flexibility, resilience, and adaptability.** Education systems need to be flexible, resilient, and adaptable enough to deal constructively with individual differences. Those they serve also expect the same kind of thing from business, government, and other fields. Tokyo International School Vision Navigator Patrick Newell says "personalization equals the opportunity to get involved in something that is interesting, engaging, and relevant."

• **Personalizing as a key to more flexible and comprehensive standards.** As pressure intensified for better student achievement, standards and high-stakes tests narrowed the focus of K-12 education. *Salon.com* quotes education historian Diane Ravitch—"When reading and math count and nothing else does, then less time and resources are devoted to non-tested subjects like the arts, science, history, civics, and so on."[99] Beware—the tyranny of the average. Average scores may go up, but many students are thankfully not *average*. Rather than focusing on winners and losers, we need to invest in helping all students succeed to the best of their ability.

• **Eagerly responding to the challenges of technology, mind-brain research, and globalization.** While these persistent forces are disrupting the environment and putting whitecaps on the calm seas of the status quo, we'd better strongly consider their implications for personalizing education. Are we drawing on the richness of *multiple sources of education* to enhance learning?

• **Making education more interesting, exciting, and related to what is important in life.** Harvard's David Perkins has described "a relevance gap" and calls for "lifeworthy" learning. He's suggests we consider what content matters in our lives today and will matter in the future—in the lives of learners.[100]

- **Becoming talent scouts.** On top of scientific research, which is vitally important, we need to use our senses to spot interests, talents, and motivations, then build on them. Like good detectives, we need to always be on the lookout for clues. Those clues (or connections) are all around us if we're looking and listening.

- **Moving beyond a "scoreboard mentality."** We need to resist the temptation to believe that progress in education can be reduced to the reporting of a simple set of numbers, like box scores for baseball, football, hockey, soccer, and other sports. Veteran teacher *Milde Waterfall* asks, "How do we define, measure, and monitor teacher/student success in a pluralistic society?"

- **More implications for personalization.** While we're personalizing, we need to also be sure we are emphasizing teamwork. Educators and society should be keenly aware that good education is firmly linked to concerns about equity and adequacy of funding. Assessment should be used to provide good information for improving education, not to sort out winners and losers, or give us an oversimplified scoreboard.

Trend 13: Ingenuity. *Flashes of Insight!*

Trend: Releasing ingenuity and stimulating creativity will become primary responsibilities of education and society.

> "Imagination is more important than knowledge. Knowledge is limited. Imagination encircles the world."
> *Albert Einstein[101]*

Ingenuity
Turning it on. Tuning it up. Turning it off.

It's jaw dropping! Every day, each of us wakes up to a stark reality—the challenges we face aren't yielding to business as usual. Vast knowledge is good, and we highly recommend it, but it doesn't substitute for an ample dose of creativity, imagination, mindfulness, and problem solving. If you don't believe it, scan the employment ads. Trying to blow the lid off standardized test scores is a goal worth pursuing, but most of us will only be able to capitalize on the achievement if we have well oiled thinking, reasoning, and contemplation skills and the ability to perform across disciplines.

Intellectual Entrepreneurs. We read books, visit exhibitions, go to movies, click on web sites, or immerse ourselves in social media, largely because they pique our imaginations. Most of us are transfixed by stories about those who pioneered an idea or broke new ground. In varying degrees, that pioneering spirit lies deep within each of us. It's an entrepreneur, just waiting to see the light of day—hoping to make it economically or just make a positive difference. It's up to everyone, certainly every educator, to spot, encourage, and help develop the ingenuity that is in each of us and all around us.

Knowledge Creation and Breakthrough Thinking
Making Connections across Disciplines

Big questions. How can we help our students learn and think across disciplines? Who is paying attention to the connective tissue, the white spaces, and the natural links between and among disciplines and across an organization? When we fire up our smartphones or tablets, do we focus only on those things that interest us most, or do we reach out to discover how what we see and hear might impact others? Do we see things *in context*?

The answers to these and dozens of similar questions are urgent as we conceive of and pursue our future. In fact, it is our ability to think, plan, and work across disciplines that has been a driver for our economy and civil society. As specialized as we might be, all of us, whether we like it or not—will live interdisciplinary lives.

"Schools are fairly good at promoting the acquisition of information," says Avis Glaze, president of Edu-quest International in Canada. "The focus now has to shift quickly to knowledge creation and breakthrough thinking, which support a culture of ingenuity and creativity."

Why Ingenuity and Creativity? Why Now?

Releasing ingenuity, stimulating creativity, and encouraging imagination are not just nice things to do. Instead, they are essential to the advancement and very survival of both our economy and our civil society, wherever we live on the planet.

Sir Kenneth Robinson, who has U.K. origins, is a widely known creativity expert. He argues, "We are educating people out of their creativity."[102] Sir Ken makes the case that creativity is as important as literacy, but students are conditioned to be frightened of doing anything wrong. "All over the world," he submits, "formal education systematically suppresses creative thinking and flexibility." Ellen Winner, psychology chair and director of the Arts and Mind Lab at Boston College, says she has found positive risk-taking common among the most creative students.[103]

New ideas are not, by their very nature, necessarily threatening. Some could even put us on the leading edge of the future. Knowing how to deal with ideas in context and understanding a process for innovation are becoming a leadership essential.

Take Time for Reflection. What seems like an exponentially growing number of educators are talking about the importance of "reflection" for their students. However, consumed by daily demands both inside and outside the system and constantly pursued by an array of communication technologies and stacks of requirements, creativity could become a victim. Educators need to reflect on approaches to teaching and learning that will get students ready for life in a changing and challenging world.

Uncork Ingenuity, Give Permission. A good first step in releasing ingenuity and stimulating creativity, in ourselves and others, is simply letting go. Please remember this—You don't need authority to give someone else permission to pursue their talents.

The Arts, Helping Us Think, Create, Imagine, and Innovate. We are surrounded and consumed by the arts. Sometimes we don't even notice. Music, dance, musical theater, the visual arts, design, creative writing, and many other art forms stimulate our thinking and fire our imaginations. They can also reinforce achievement in other subjects.

A Few More Thoughts about Thinking

In canvassing various groups about what they think are "the most important things for students to learn," *thinking* usually works its way to the top of the list, according to Project Zero's David Perkins.[104] "Good thinkers have a tendency to identify and investigate problems, to probe assumptions, to seek reasons, and to be reflective." [105]

Arthur Costa is an emeritus professor at California State University in Sacramento and co-author of an ASCD series devoted to *Habits of Mind*. He suggests five themes for any "thought-filled curriculum: learning to think, thinking to learn, thinking together, thinking about our own thinking, and thinking big." Costa recommends frequent questions to enliven thinking.[106]

For example, we might pose ongoing questions such as: Why do you feel that way? What opinions do you think other people might have about it? How could we solve the problem? What should we do first? What process did you use to form that opinion? How did you make your decision? In a world intent on quickly coming up with all the answers, many people are concerned about whether we're asking the right questions.

Implications for Education and Society—*Ingenuity, Knowledge Creation, and Breakthrough Thinking*

Social and economic challenges, discoveries in neuroscience, massive developments in technology, globalization, political upheaval, the urgency of invention, the need for new industries and jobs, and a host of other issues and concerns are shaking the world's foundations. Everything that impacts the world impacts schools and colleges. If it doesn't, there's a good chance someone is out of touch. Implications?

• **Pursuing active learning, project-based and real-world education, learning through inquiry, differentiated instruction, and learning across disciplines.** While "sit and listen" may still be important, engagement has become essential. Classrooms are turning into hubs for active learning, project-based education, real-world education, learning through inquiry, and learning across disciplines.

• **Expecting the focus on education to become more intense.** During tumultuous times, especially following economic downturns, the eyes of the world focus on education. A challenge for educators will be to understand that focus as a *growing demand* rather than as *criticism*.

• **Nurturing creativity, imagination, ingenuity, mindfulness, and flexibility.** Flexibility will be essential for our political and educational systems around the world to embrace moving from a laser focus on *what we already know* to *discovering and creating new knowledge*. That will mean paying increased attention to cognitive research, staying close to forces impacting society, and personalizing our approach to education. Futures Council 21 member Keith Marty looks for "public and private incentives [that] will lead to a new surge of American genius and new ideas."

• **Becoming more knowledgeable about Mind, Brain, and Education (MBE).** Relatively speaking, MBE is a new field and will likely become even more prominent. It encompasses educational neuroscience, philosophy, linguistics, pedagogy, developmental psychology, and other areas.[107]

- **Cultivating Thinking and Reasoning Skills.** Critical and creative thinking are essential. An understanding of logic can help us maneuver inductive and deductive reasoning. Creative or lateral thinking can help us think outside the box and generate flashes of insight. Here's another thought. Ask students if what they've learned today has triggered any ideas for them.

- **Opening Our Minds as Leaders.** Both elected and selected political and community leaders will likely be expected to have a level of open-mindedness, creativity, and ingenuity as we confront challenges that have massive social and economic impact.

- **Making Innovation a Priority.** Remember that cultivating invention, innovation, and entrepreneurial activity should be front and center in discussions about a community's or a country's future.

- **Preparing and Encouraging Inventive People.** Education systems will be expected to turn out inventive people who have finely developed thinking, reasoning, and problem-solving skills and a capacity to use creativity and imagination.

Trend 14: Depth, Breadth, and Purposes of Education.
What do we need to know?

Trend: The breadth, depth, and purposes of education will constantly be clarified to meet the needs of a fast-changing world.

Zooming Out... to the Big Picture

Ask this question, "What are the purposes of education?" In reality, it's a discussion that should never leave the agenda. Of course, purposes get wrapped up in politics, special interests, biases, economic arguments, and often-firm viewpoints.

Some say education should stick to teaching the 3-Rs. Others submit that the purpose is broader, and should include getting students ready for productive lives as contributors to the economy and civil society. Somehow, we have wrapped our philosophy and purposes of education around a debate that helped shape schools for an Industrial Age. Now, we're moving into a Global Knowledge/Information Age. To the frustration of growing numbers of educators, we are too often faced with the prospect of preparing our students for the future—constrained by a mentality and infrastructure from another time.

Purposes of Education

Just to get the discussion started, please let me propose five purposes for education:
- **Citizenship.** Create good citizens of a family, community, country, and world.
- **Employability.** Help students develop the knowledge, skills, talents, and habits of mind they need to be employable, whether they are self-employed or aspire to work inside an organization in the for-profit or not-for-profit sector.

- **Interesting Lives.** Encourage students to see the connection between what they are being asked to learn and real life, noting that, generally, the more we know and the broader our experience, the more interesting life becomes.
- **Releasing Ingenuity that is Already There.** Discover the personal ingenuity of students, their interests, skills, abilities, and aspirations, and build on them.
- **Stimulating Imagination, Creativity, and Inventiveness.** Recognizing and cultivating the creative nature of students.

Breadth and Depth
Getting Past the Gathering Narrowness

Unfortunately, we've been highly successful at fractionating the purposes of education. *Subjects* have often been forced to compete with each other for attention. That situation has left little or no room in the conversation for the bigger picture. The time has come to do some breadth and depth perception.

Captives of the Cognitive. The pressures of academic standards, testing, college readiness, expansion of knowledge, habits, and demands of several disciplines continue to fuel an unending debate about depth vs. breadth in education. Cognitive knowledge and skills are deeply important, but, alone, they aren't enough. Thinking, creating, imagining, innovating, communicating, and working across disciplines is and will always be flat-out essential if we hope to build a better future for our economy, our civil society, and ourselves.

What we teach and how we teach it has to be aligned with the fast-changing needs of society. We need to consider the emergence of new technologies and a growing restlessness that involves everything from jobs and the economy to systemic innovation and international competition.

What do we all need to know and be able to do?

Right off the bat, you undoubtedly have some firm opinions about what we will all need to know and be able to do if we hope to be poised for the future. Let's hold our horses for a few minutes while we explore how some people and institutions have or likely would have responded to a similar challenge.

For example, in ancient Athens, *Plato's Academy* focused on art, science, literature, music, astronomy, biology, mathematics, political theory, philosophy, and other pursuits, such as Socratic Dialogues. While *Horace Mann* called for practical knowledge and a moral compass, *John Dewey* led the charge for building a relationship between education and democratic life. The historic *Seven Cardinal Principles*, developed in 1918, included: health, a command of fundamental processes, worthy home membership, vocation, civic education, worthy use of leisure, and ethical character. Harvard developmental psychologist and professor *Howard Gardner's Five Minds for the Future* describes the disciplined mind, the synthesizing mind, the creating mind, the respectful mind, and the ethical mind.[108]

A 2002 *No Child Left Behind* Act focused primarily on reading and math. In 2009, a presidential STEM initiative zeroed in on science, technology, engineering, and math. Then, in 2010, Common Core Standards were developed aimed at improving student performance in English/language arts and mathematics.

Twenty Targets for the 21ˢᵗ Century

Based on these and other insights, we've developed a preliminary list of "Twenty Targets for the 21ˢᵗ Century," aiming at general categories of what we all need to know and be able to do. In some cases, that means at least a working knowledge.

Those general targets include: communication; science; technology; mathematics; engineering and architecture; thinking and reasoning; imagination, creativity, and innovation; knowledge creation and breakthrough thinking; the arts; judgment, ethics, and character; civil discourse and ability to overcome narrowness and polarization; employability skills; leadership and management; economics and personal finance; social and behavioral science; civic knowledge, skills, and dispositions; global/international knowledge and skills; environmental and planetary security; health, well-being, life skills, and work-life balance; and futures processes and forecasting.

Consider this a work in progress, and use this list to spur an ongoing conversation. Over time, our lists might change a bit, since the world doesn't stop. Neither does our need to be flexible and consider new ideas.

Fitting a Broad and Deep Education...*into a Crowded Curriculum*

One way to demonstrate the law of supply and demand is to compare what people want us to teach (demand) with the number of days, hours, sometimes knowledge or experience that we have to teach it (supply). It's a perennial concern; it won't go away.

After all, every day the earth spins, the story of history gets longer and more complex. Scientific discoveries and technological advances seem to pile one on another. "We need to educate about the known, and we need to also educate for the unknown," Project Zero's David Perkins has said.

Perkins suggests that, as we consider what we teach, we should ask whether it is "lifeworthy." He points out that, since knowledge continues to grow and we can't teach everything in depth, we should, in some cases, use "smart sampling." In teaching history, Perkins suggests a form of *post holing*, focusing on certain events or periods that open the door to "rich cases, works, and artifacts" that can help us learn lessons about democracy, discontent, diseases, and an array of big ideas.

Implications for Education and Society—*Depth, Breadth, and Purposes of Education*

With an explosion in what we need to know and be able to do, we're naturally confronted by the issue of narrowness and shallowness vs. depth and breadth. That brings us to the question, "What are the implications of this trend for education and society?" Here are a few of those implications for your consideration. Please think of others.

• **Keeping Purpose, Breadth, and Depth Always on the Agenda.** Seriously bring this philosophical, but also very real, set of topics out of the closet and place them squarely on the continuing agenda for discussion, system-wide and community-wide. Make the schools a crossroads and central convening point for the community as people consider substantive issues.

• **Overcoming the Temptation to Narrow the Curriculum.** Elected and appointed officials should understand that narrowing the curriculum could also narrow the short-term and longer-term possibilities for their community, state, or nation. Decisions based on short-term political gain vs. longer-term benefit for society can do damage to the economy and quality of life that could take decades to repair.

• **Stimulating Conversations across Disciplines.** Much of what we need to know today and will need to know tomorrow is in the spaces between and among disciplines. Within schools and colleges, educators will need to stimulate intense and energizing conversations exploring cross-disciplinary approaches to teaching and learning.

• **Considering What is Lifeworthy.** The collective mass of knowledge is expanding exponentially. However, the number of hours in a school day remains about the same as it has been for years. As we continue to face an even more crowded curriculum, discussions within and across disciplines should, as a matter of course, constantly consider what is, "lifeworthy."[109]

• **Conducting Research Projects.** When appropriate, encourage students to undertake research projects that will help them discover the breadth and depth of what they are studying. Use the interest students develop as part of those projects to instill further curiosity and persistence in exploring both questions and answers.

Trend 15: Polarization
Don't confuse me with the facts.
My mind is already made up.

Trend: Polarization and narrowness will, of
necessity, bend toward reasoned discussion,
evidence, and consideration of varying points
of view.

> **"When we understand the other fellow's viewpoint, and he
> understands ours, then we can sit down and work out
> our differences."**
> *Harry S. Truman, Former U.S. President*

Grouping people around two extremes can produce an entertaining
television program. However, in the real world, the lack of willingness
or ability to reasonably deliberate, to discuss and debate serious issues
can lead to constant conflict, gridlock, acts of terror, and even war.
Reliability is undermined; evidence is ignored; reasonable alternatives
never see the light of day; and progress suffers potentially fatal wounds.

When an organization, community, or country cannot address important concerns because it is chronically fractionated, problems remain unsolved. Then they intensify. Key ideas don't make the agenda
and become drowning victims in a sea of narrowness. When feuding
factions and unending contentious battles take precedence over progress, communities and nations fall behind. The common good takes a
back seat to gridlock.

The world is moving beyond vertical, top-down, sometimes dog-
matic and partisan approaches to problem solving. Those who insist
on simply having it their way because that's the way their contributors
or clients want it are missing something that is very important. We
now live in a collaborative, lateral, networked world, connected 24/7.
Those who, out of hand, ignore other points of view may be blindsid-
ing themselves—playing a role that is so defensive (or offensive) that

thoughtful and creative people with new ideas simply go over, around, or through them. A few might even become competitors who tout their willingness to collaborate.

Polarization. What is it?

In his *Dictionary of Cultural Literacy*, conservative education philosopher E.D. Hirsch defines polarization this way: "In politics, the grouping of opinions around two extremes: As the debate continued, the...members were polarized into warring factions."[110] On the street, it might sound like this: "It's us versus them." "You're either with us or against us." "Take my word for it, it's black or white. There are no shades of gray." "Forget about principle. All that matters is whether we win."

What's at Stake? *Civility*

A major driver of education is a commitment to get students ready to become engaged, contributing members of civil society. That should mean they understand the importance of reasoned discussion; that they know how to gather, consider, and present evidence; and that they have some commitment to comprehending, not necessarily accepting, a variety of points of view.

Granted, factions are a normal part of any society. Throughout history, they have kept the flame of liberty burning. However, even with all of our sophisticated interactive social media, way too many of us are moving from talking *with* each other to talking *past* each other.

Our future, even our existence, could depend on our working together. Rather than truly getting anything big done, Thomas Friedman suggests, "we have to generate so many compromises with so many interest groups," that we end up with "suboptimal solutions that are only the sum of all interest groups."[111]

Perhaps the greatest casualty of an over-polarized society and world is that it keeps us from putting divergent ideas and information together to create new knowledge that could enrich economies and civil societies.

Implications for Education and the Whole of Society—*Polarization*
• **Identify and teach the basic skills of a civil society.** Education is challenged to bring civility to fractious, sometimes gridlocked or warring communities or whole societies. Civility is, of course, essential to our pursuit of a legitimate, sustainable future.

What are the skills, attitudes, and behaviors we need to be declared "civil?" A few might include: empathy; ethical behavior; respect for others despite our differences; the ability to think, reason, and solve problems; an ability to resolve conflict peacefully and democratically; and a commitment to engage people in discussions and listen to their ideas. Civic education is essential to development of a *civic temperament.*

• **Start the discussion of civility with hard questions.** Thoughtfully and honestly involve diverse groups in discussing answers to a few key questions, such as: Are students prepared to become engaged, contributing members of a truly civil society? Do they know how to gather, consider, and present evidence, then build a viable plan? Do they have a commitment to comprehending, not necessarily accepting, a variety of points of view? Are they capable of separating truth from fiction? Wheat from chaff?

• **Model civility and engagement in how we teach.** When we thoughtfully engage students, we send a message of respect. That's among reasons why active learning across disciplines; project-based learning; real-world education; learning through inquiry; and thinking, reasoning, and problem solving skills are important.

Authors Note: The tug between polarization and reasoned discussion, evidence, and consideration of varying point of view is a very serious matter. Deepening divisions created by an all-or-nothing approach to dealing with every issue or problem, with little regard for the common good, is likely unsustainable.

Trend 16: Authority.
By the power vested in me...

Trend: A spotlight will fall on how people gain authority and use it.

> **"If your actions inspire others to dream more, learn more, do more, and become more, you are a leader."**
> *Former U.S. President John Quincy Adams*

Martin Luther King, Jr., Nelson Mandela, and Mahatma Gandhi are among 20th and 21st century leaders who are revered for their courage and unyielding devotion to justice. Their larger-than-life examples stood taller than any high office or narrow self interest. They earned what many call *moral authority*.

Authority
Declared? Conferred? Assumed? Earned?

Does education prepare us for the world or just provide an introduction? Do we respect the school of life? Should authority simply be declared or conferred or should it *also* be earned? Should connectedness, creativity, thoughtfulness, productivity, ethical behavior, and a steadfast commitment to the common good trump privilege, title, and position? Is genuine leadership more important than dictum? Does merit count?

World history and current events blaze with examples of declared, conferred, or assumed authority that has led to authoritarianism, anger, suffering, and, in some cases, revolt and overthrow.

The *good news*? As we move more deeply into the 21st century, it's pretty clear that the parade of marching orders is out ...and collaboration is in. We need the vertical but it should be balanced with the horizontal.

> **"A spotlight on authority may reflect a generational trend of questioning assumptions."**
> *Frank Kwan*

Authority, Authorities, Authoritative, Authoritarian
What's the Difference?

We're generally relieved when we hear that a car accident or home break-in has been reported to the *authorities*. On a massive range of issues, we want those who have been elected or appointed to various positions to act on our behalf. That's true in both the public and private sectors. We delegate *authority* to certain people or groups and expect them to carry out their responsibilities fairly. Most of us hope that those who have been given responsibility and authority to govern and enforce will be able to govern themselves. In government, we try to somewhat disperse authority through separation of powers. We refer to some people as *authoritative*, not necessarily because they hold a certain title or position, but because of their depth of knowledge or experience.

Then, we come to *authoritarianism*. That's dicier. One definition: "blind submission to authority." Another: "a concentration of power" in a way that is not responsible to the people.[112] Our hope is for *servant leaders* who are dedicated to the common good.

Implications for Education and Society—*Authority*

• Students, educators, business and government leaders, and others need to understand the foundations of inclusive decision making and how to legitimately use authority in achieving the common good.

• Authority might be included in discussions across many areas of a school or college curriculum, including: social studies, civic education, government, history, communication, the sciences, technology, leadership, media literacy, and other courses.

• Across disciplines, students and others in the community will need to have opportunities to experience public engagement and teamwork. All might learn to identify issues and problems, conduct research, develop plans of action, suggest public policy, and earn public consent.

• Students at every level should receive a grounding in foundational principles that are basic to democracy, such as authority, justice, privacy, and responsibility. Each should be able to find a balance between arrogance and empathy, understand human and civil rights, and learn how to identify benefits and consequences of their own actions.

• All will need to understand the consequences of corruption and authority that has been misdirected for the benefit of the few at the expense of the many. A position of authority should be understood as a position of responsibility and service, not simply a source of personal privilege.

• Preparation programs and ongoing professional development in every field should prepare people to exercise legitimate future-focused leadership in a fast-changing world.

Trend 17: Ethics.
Let's try to do the right thing.

Trend: Scientific discoveries and societal realities will force widespread ethical choices.

> **"The first step in the evolution of ethics is a sense of solidarity with other human beings."**
> *Albert Schweitzer*

Ethics! What does it mean?

While ethics may mean different things to different people, we'll let *Webster's New Collegiate Dictionary* be our arbiter. "Ethics," according to *Webster's*, is "the discipline of dealing with what is good and bad and with moral duty and obligation." It's "a theory or system of moral values."[113]

Some refer to ethics as a set of guidelines, a code of conduct, a basis for professionalism, and a form of behavior. Many agree that ethics often takes over when we reach the limits of the law, since some things might be technically legal but still don't seem appropriate. One thing is certain: When we're faced with a massive breach of ethics, everything else on our agenda takes second place.

Then, there is corruption. In defining it, the State Secretariat for Economic Affairs (SECO) in Switzerland, notes that, "Corrupt practices can range from small favors in anticipation of future advantage to the payment of large sums of money to senior members of governments."[114]

Ethics can involve what we say and do, how we say and do it, and what we decide not to say and do. Among the best safeguards in guiding our ethical behavior is a commitment to treating people with respect rather than imposing our will without consulting them. Just to provide fair warning: The minute we stray from the Golden Rule, *doing unto others as you would have them do unto you*, we're headed directly toward *an eye for an eye and a tooth for a tooth.*

Pragmatic? Expedient? Ethical? How Important is the Ethical?

Pragmatic: "Whatever works." *Expedient*: "Whatever is easiest." *Ethical*: "What's the right thing to do?" We know that the pragmatic and expedient can be ethical, but we should ask ourselves how any of our actions will impact the lives of others.

How important is an understanding of ethics? The response is generally, "It could not be more important. It's absolutely essential!" Then comes the challenge. How do we develop ethical behavior? In theory, educators hone a sense of ethics through precept and example, but do we really do it? If we do, why? If we don't, why not?

"Without moral courage, our brightest virtues rust from lack of use. With it, we build piece by piece a more ethical world."
Rushworth Kidder, Founder, Institute for Global Ethics[115]

Ethical Challenges and Breaches
They Get Our Attention!

Without naming names, here are a few situations that have captured our attention. Feel free to use them as mini-scenarios or as ethics discussion starters.

• A newspaper runs a photo of a man being struck by a subway train. Should the journalist have just recorded the incident or tried to rescue the person in peril?[116]

• A celebrated bicyclist, who won numerous world titles, is investigated for use of performance-enhancing drugs. After repeated denials, he admits the truth. Should he have retained his titles and medals?

• Educators are accused of altering student answer sheets used with high stakes tests as a way to give the appearance of higher than average achievement scores. How do you react to these incidents?

• A classmate tells you confidentially that he plans to bring a gun to school tomorrow. He adds, "You'll keep this quiet if you know what's good for you. Don't be a snitch." What will you do? When?

• A small group of young people taunts a student who is new to the school. The harassment spreads from name-calling and intimidation in hallways to scandalous but false rumors online. What should we do?

Each of us may want to spend some time thinking about the need for honor and a moral compass to get past an attitude summed up by, "The problem is not violating a code of ethics. The problem is getting caught."

> "To be persuasive we must be believable; to be believable we must be credible; to be credible we must be truthful."
> *Edward R. Murrow, American Broadcast Journalist[117]*

Markers on the Road to Ethics Education

Why is ethical behavior so important for people and organizations of all types, especially education institutions? Four possible answers: trust, reputation, credibility, and our ability to get the support we need for educating our students.

Michael Josephson, president of the Josephson Foundation, home of *Character Counts*, focuses on the "Six Pillars of Character: trustworthiness, respect, responsibility, fairness, caring, and citizenship."[118] Josephson adds, "The ethical person should do more than he is required to do, and less than he is allowed to."[119]

Ethics is often taught through *precept* and *example*. In short, we are generally most successful at delivering lessons in ethics through building an understanding of ethical principles and reinforcing them with real-life stories and role-playing.

> "We need to find common ground on values across our many areas of diversity, create humane and productive workplaces, and build peaceful and inclusive communities."
> *Avis Glaze*

Ethical Issues Facing Today's Students

Can we truly say a student is well educated without a firm grasp of ethical behavior? Probably not. As they move into positions of leadership and take on their role as citizens, today's students will be faced with some of the most monumental ethical dilemmas of all time. A few of the issues they likely will face include:

- The need for adequate, accessible, fresh, clean water.
- Honesty and transparency in financial and other organizations.
- Computer and social media ethics, ranging from hacking into private, organizational, or governmental files to cyberbullying, sexting, implanting viruses, and recklessness in the use of technologies, such as texting while driving.
- Investments that *are* or *are not* made in seeking the prevention and cures of major diseases and avoiding pandemics.

"Power is given to you by others. It is not yours; it is in trust with you and it is a great responsibility. Power is to be used for the benefit of those whose trustee you are."
Mahatma Gandhi

Human Rights... in Perspective

"The notion of human rights builds on the idea of a shared humanity," according to Mei-Ying Tang of Taipei Municipal University of Education. She adds, "Human rights are not derived from citizenship or nationality but are the entitlement of every human being. In this sense, the concept of human rights is a universal and uniting idea."[120]

"The Morning Question: What good shall I do this day? The Evening Question: What good have I done today?"
Ben Franklin's Two Daily Questions[121]

Implications for Education and Society—*Ethics*

- **Modeling ethical leadership.** Education institutions, by their very nature, are expected to be paragons of ethical behavior, since they play such a central role in modeling that type of behavior for students.
- **Including an ethics component in every course.** In any class, daily or weekly, a teacher might present this challenge, "Think about what we've discussed today (or this week). What are the ethical implications for us as individuals, for our school, for our community, for our country, for the world?"

- **Expanding programs in thinking and reasoning skills as well as civic and character education.** As students develop their critical and creative thinking skills, they will be better prepared to observe pros and cons as they make choices and solve problems, whether in school, on the job, or as a citizen on the front lines of society.

- **Dealing with cyber-ethics, as well as physical and intellectual enhancements.** The cyber-world brings its own panoply of ethical challenges that educators will continue to address. Among them are cyberbullying, identity and privacy concerns, hacking of confidential school district employee or student records, and a host of other issues.

Schools and colleges have dealt with the issue of performance-enhancing drugs, primarily in athletics. Future policy issues might include the use of pharmaceuticals or supplements that are seen as intelligence enhancements.

- **Getting beyond arrogance and moving toward empathy.** Too often, people willfully do things to benefit themselves at the expense of many others. A lack of empathy and compassion breeds arrogance.

- **Additional Implications of Ethics Trend.** Among further implications, the need for professional development and an expectation that we will adhere to codes of ethics.

Trend 18: Continuous Improvement
You ain't seen nuthin' yet.

Trend: The status quo will yield to continuous improvement and reasoned progress.

‖ **"A bad system will beat a good person every time."**
‖ *W. Edwards Deming*

Good Today...
Even Better Tomorrow!

Resistance to something new is likely as old as humanity itself. However, in a world of quantum physics and exponential change, simply digging in our heels and passionately defending the status quo won't cut it.

Let's face it, if we were perfect yesterday, we probably aren't perfect today, because the world changed overnight. Two questions: "Are we committed to continuous improvement?" and "Are we flexible enough to adjust?"

People today expect and demand quality, effectiveness, and service. In the past, an organization might get by with defending the status quo or going for the quick fix—the band aid approach. Now, in an impatient world, people want products and services that work, meet their needs, and are delivered on time.

Principles of Quality Improvement

The principles of quality improvement, unleashed by statistician and consultant W. Edwards Deming, were summarized in his classic book, *Out of Crisis*. Included are: developing a constancy of purpose toward improvement; stopping dependence on inspection by building quality into the product in the first place; improving the system of production and service; ensuring that leadership helps people do a better job; breaking down barriers among departments; substituting leadership for standards; getting rid of barriers that rob people of their pride of workmanship; changing responsibilities to reflect quality rather than sheer numbers; offering on-the-job training and opportunities for education and self-improvement; and driving fear from the organization.[122]

Caution on the Road to Continuous Improvement.

It's not easy staying ahead of the curve. In the private sector, the verdict often shows up in sales reports and the success of competitors. In the public sector, it can appear as people who are dissatisfied and demanding that the system change.

Of course, a laser focus on process can lead us toward doing the wrong things even more effectively. We live in an age of the end run. If we don't think an institution is meeting our expectations, we'll very likely run around it, through it, or over it. If an organization's decisions don't make it easier for people to get an even better product or service on time, they'll either *turn to* the competition or *become* the competition.

Implications for Education and Society—*Continuous Improvement*

All education institutions should reflect a spirit of constant renewal, exude positive and constructive energy, get their communities and staffs on board, seriously listen to the wisdom that surrounds them, and offer outstanding future-focused professional development. They will need to work with staff, governance, and community to turn blocking cultures into enabling cultures, and maintain flexibility.

• **Education institutions will be expected to be vibrant, flexible, and effective.** Governing boards, administrators, teachers, and communities need to be key players in helping the system become even better tomorrow than it is today, no matter how great that might be.

• **A commitment to continuous improvement should add intellectual energy and value to the system and everyone in it.** No education system will be able to safely say that it has "arrived." The needs of society and possibilities for education multiply, meaning satisfaction will come from staying ahead of the curve, not kicking off our shoes and declaring we're the best.

• **Quality and continuous improvement will find their way into the classroom.** To be prepared for a demanding, complex, but invigorating world, students will need to understand and get hands-on experience with principles of quality. Active learning pumps energy into the classroom, making it a place where "what we learn is connected to the real world."

- **Earning the opportunity to serve.** Organizations take up space. They are there because they've accepted responsibility for providing what they hope will be an essential cluster of services. They create value. Others may also want to occupy that space. Every organization must constantly prove that it is earning the opportunity to serve.

- **A commitment to continuous improvement *should* become basic, but the system *should not* stymie imagination, creativity, invention, and innovation.** Efforts to achieve "zero defects" in our processes should not blindside us to evolving wants and needs. Again, to freeze is to fail.

- **Citizens, customers, and clients will expect outstanding service.** While all will insist on product quality, they will generally develop zero tolerance for hassles and inefficiency and insist on knowing what value a product or service will add to their lives.

Trend 19: Poverty.
Poverty makes us all poor.

Trend: Understanding will grow that sustained poverty is expensive, debilitating, and unsettling.

> **"Mama may have, papa may have, but God bless the child that's got his own."**
> *Billie Holiday and Arthur Herzog, Jr.*[123]

The Many Faces of Poverty

How do we measure poverty? Generally, we compare levels of income. We declare that people who make less than a certain amount of money are poor. In a quantifying society, that seems reasonable to most of us, and it probably is. However, poverty is deeper than numbers on a well-designed chart. It is a condition that impacts the lives of real people.

By 2012, when the Great Recession seemed to be winding down, 22 percent of all children under 18 in the U.S. — approximately 16 million—were living in poverty.[124] Raise your hand if you would like to walk a mile in their shoes. Imagine feeling trapped in the grip of social and economic peril with only rumors of *opportunity*.

One worrisome concern that should command our attention is the persistence of *sustained poverty*. We find it in our individual communities, in our nations, and worldwide. It's a situation that almost seems to be inherited. From generation to generation, it increases exponentially. For too many, except the most robust, poverty can drain the human spirit and weaken the body. It can become devastating as *hope* becomes a long forgotten dream.

While some people are born into poverty, others are limited by discrimination or a lack of educational opportunity. Still others might have been marginalized by a changing or softening economy, down-sizing, mistakes, foreclosure, bankruptcy, the loss of a job, illness, an accident, low expectations, or an absence of mentoring and support. Consider dilemmas such as: a lack of adequate and affordable health care; limited access to a predictable, healthy food supply or diet; low birthweight babies and inadequate prenatal care; family stress or break-up; and a vast array of other social and economic conditions.

Globally, in 2010, the World Bank estimated that 1.2 billion people on our planet were living in *extreme poverty*—under $1.25 a day—and nearly 2.5 billion were living on less than $2 a day.[125]

Too often, we turn a blind eye to the lost potential that surrounds us. If we hope to have a future, then we need to be sure those who are coming up behind us can continue, with a sense of dignity, the climb toward even more productive and fulfilling lives. We need to remember that if one person is poor, we are all poorer for it.

The Cost of Neglect

For too many students, poverty has a way of impacting school achievement. It shows up in standardized test scores, student grades, dropout rates, and both college entrance and completion. A soft econ-omy raised the hurdles for educators trying to move that needle.

Ensuring equal educational opportunity for all, despite social, eco-nomic, and other factors, is an ongoing quest. Attention to this critical issue heats up and then wanes. At the federal level, the historic Ele-mentary and Secondary Education Act (ESEA) focuses on the needs of disadvantaged students.

Poverty and Equal Opportunity. In an *Education Week* Commen-tary, Michael Rebell and Jessica Wolff of the Campaign for Education-al Equity at Teachers College, Columbia University, declare, "America does not have a general education crisis, we have a poverty crisis."[126] Are we truly ready to address the equal opportunity crisis, even if we are among the advantaged?

Over time, a groundswell has been rising for even better and more far-reaching early childhood education and a renewed commitment to equal educational opportunity for all.

Share of the World's Private Consumption

In 2005, the world's richest 20 percent accounted for 76.6 percent of all private consumption. The world's middle 60 percent accounted for 21.9 percent of all private consumption. The world's poorest 20 percent accounted for 1.5 percent of all private consumption.
World Bank Development Indicators 2008[127]

> "Shameful child poverty levels call for urgent and persistent action. It's way past time to eliminate epidemic child poverty and the child suffering, stress, homelessness, and miseducation it spawns."
> *Marian Wright Edelman, Children's Defense Fund, Huffington Post*[128]

Implications for Education and Society—*Poverty*

• **Understanding the history and consequences of sustained poverty.** Schools and communities need a heightened understanding of the role poverty has played throughout history and the challenges it poses for the future. If we choose not to learn from history, then we may, indeed, be forced to relive it.

• **Offering education programs that prepare people to avoid or overcome poverty.** If we are *not* in poverty, we need to understand how to avoid it. If we are *in* poverty, we need to understand how we might possibly get and stay out of it. From dwindling retirement savings to job losses and home foreclosures, the Great Recession of the early 2000s pushed thousands of people into financial uncertainty. Their future and the futures of their children were threatened.

In addition to equal opportunity, a response to this challenge is that we need better economic education and an even deeper grasp of personal financial knowledge and skills, a commitment to ethical behavior, resilience, and an education that is broad and deep enough to apply in a variety of future jobs and careers and in life.

• **Motivating students by personalizing education, not just aiming for higher average test scores.** We must be sure that we don't lose our focus on those who end up on the lower end of the curve. All students need an education that is broad and deep, not just a scaled down curriculum that is more easily tested.

Trend 20: Scarcity vs. Abundance. *What's enough?*

Trend: Scarcity will help us rethink our view of abundance.

> **"Necessity is the mother of invention."**
> *Source Unknown. Often attributed to Plato*

The Overwhelming Power of Needs and Wants

What is it about us? We're captivated by the struggle. We lean forward and soak up stories about people who have overcome adversity, beaten the odds, made it through a storm, found a legitimate way to go from rags to riches, or simply just survived.

A struggle we carry with us every day is balancing our needs and wants. If we simply *want* something, we make a case, even to justify it for ourselves, that we really *need* it.

Scarcity

Some cultures thrive on scarcity. They take pride in it. You might hear a story something like this, "Times were tough, but we made do with what we had." A lot of us wear our scarcity as a badge of honor, as an expression of our beliefs, or as a way to reduce our footprint on the ecosystem.

Genuine scarcity is not a myth. In fact, it is a stark reality for millions of people every day. That could mean a scarcity of nourishing food, clean water, adequate health care, safety and security, arable land, or energy to power transportation and industry.

Some communities and parts of the world are left with a scarcity of know-how and an unstable civil society because of inequity in education, injustice, war, or a lack of opportunity. When a level of scarcity is tolerable, that's one thing. When it isn't, when people lack basics, such as nutritious food, clean drinking water, electricity, opportunity for education, and hope, that's something else.

Respect for the Natural World

Realize it or not, we are surrounded by abundance that flows from the natural world—air to breathe; energy from the sun; plant life that sustains us; even bees that help pollinate our crops.[129] A challenge we face is to live in harmony with the natural world. If we don't, it could cost us big time, even our survival.

Scarcities of Our Own Creation

Often, potential abundance is turned to scarcity because we've made bad choices in our financial or in our personal lives. The Great Recession is another story. Except for the wealthy, nest eggs were depleted. People who hoped for a comfortable retirement continued to work or looked for part time jobs. On top of that reality, working families were taking a flurry of hits, such as foreclosures and escalating energy costs.

While millions worldwide live without electricity, an abundance of renewable energy is all around us, if we have the political will and sense of common purpose that we need to pursue it. Research and development can lead to new ubiquitous technologies that can help turn scarcity into abundance.

Yet, in reality, some things are scarce because we just can't pay the price. At some point, the transference of scarcity to those who can least afford it has to stop. It's unsustainable. What should we do about that? How about making Internet connections available to everyone, adding microfinancing if and when it's needed, and then applauding the entrepreneurial magic.

Scarcity vs. Abundance... *In the News*

While few refer to scarcity and abundance directly, the airwaves, cyberspace, newspapers, and other media buzz with stories focusing directly on the contrast. A challenge: When we read factual information, let's consider the implications for our future and the futures of our fellow human beings. Let's try to avoid immediately seeing every fact through a partisan political lens—simply as information that confirms or disputes our preconceived notions. That's the kind of objectivity we need if we ever hope to address the issues we face as a society.

A few frequent examples: According to some reports, in 2010, the top one percent of households in the U.S. owned 35.4 percent of all privately held wealth. The bottom 80 percent had 11 percent.[130] If everyone in the world consumed like some parts of North America, we would need 4.1 earths to meet their needs.[131]

Pathways to Abundance

How can we achieve abundance? Somewhere near the top of the list is *education*. The U.S. Bureau of Labor Statistics (BLS) points out the education dividend in finding and keeping jobs. Some of us deal with scarcity by declaring, at least temporarily, that we'll pursue a *downsizing, less is more* philosophy. That might mean a more compact living space, a more fuel-efficient car, or going out to eat less often. Others join the *do-it-yourself* or *makers movement*.

Saving and investing during our peak earning years, if we can do it, might seem difficult, but it's a good choice. So is *entrepreneurship*, which can take some innovation, courage, and risk. Speaking of investing, we need to constantly improve our physical and social infrastructure. They're not an expense. They are an essential part of the foundation on which we stand.

Then, we need to *appreciate what we have*. For most of us, in our quest to overcome scarcity, we don't notice the abundance that is all around us. Despite what we're seeking, do we consider the gifts we already have in our lives?

The sense of urgency is growing to stimulate the conversation about scarcity and abundance. We need to make having that discussion a goal.

> **"The new disadvantaged may be those who have never known disadvantage. Blindsided by abundance, we might never have a chance to learn the most basic survival skills."**

Implications for Education and Society—*Scarcity vs. Abundance*

Implications of this trend are becoming more glaring, magnified by the realities of food that people *can't* afford to buy; unproductive land; the inability to obtain rare minerals that are basic to manufacturing or energy storage; or high quality education that is only available to those who can afford it. A few of the many implications include:

• **All should understand the basics of living with scarcity.** While some may only know material and financial abundance, they should be prepared to cope, in case that abundance turns to scarcity. Examples might range from financial crises leading to home foreclosures to a business leaving town, devastating a local economy.

• **Communities and whole societies should fully grasp the lost potential of talented people** who do not have opportunities for affordable, high quality education.

• **Students will need a grounding in financial literacy,** including the ability to separate needs from wants, the importance of saving and investing, and the ethical imperative of making sure as many people as possible are within reach of the golden ring.

• **Inventiveness and innovation skills** should be seen as basic, if we hope for a constantly improving economy and quality of life.

• **We need to keep in mind that scarcity may help *build character.*** However, carried to an extreme, it can turn a blind eye to possibility and deprive society of the ingenuity of those whose voices might not be heard and whose ideas may not be considered.

Trend 21: Personal Meaning and Work-Life Balance
Honey, Let's Get a Life!

Trend: More of us will seek personal meaning in our lives in response to an intense, high tech, always on, fast-moving society.

> **"Don't say you don't have enough time. You have exactly the same number of hours per day that were given to Helen Keller, Pasteur, Michelangelo, Mother Teresa, Leonardo da Vinci, Thomas Jefferson, and Albert Einstein."**
> *H. Jackson Brown, Jr.*

The Thrill of Accomplishment...
The Agony of Losing the "Life" in Work-Life Balance[132]

All around us, growing numbers of people are discovering that being wired, accessible day and night, always multitasking, can bring a jolt of satisfaction. On the other hand, if overdone, it can have devastating consequences for families and our own personal interests and well-being. For some of us, the relentless pursuit of money and thrill of accomplishment have turned us into workaholics. During tough economic times, when the job goes away, we too often discover that we've destroyed our life support system in the quest to get ahead of the Joneses. Even our greatest accomplishments can seem hollow when we have no one left in our personal lives who really cares.

Work-life balance is essential for everyone. Even children and young adults need to understand how important it will be to their futures. For many of us, it could just be a matter of *getting a life*.

Work-Family Balance
Finding Time for Life

Most of us want to be even better friends or members of our families. Maybe we want to be better members of our community. Sometimes, we think about enjoying the journey…then the smartphone rings and we're immersed. The pressures are over the top. Whether it's post-traumatic stress disorder (PTSD) or bouts of anxiety about almost anything, it's time we 'fessed up to the importance of emotional health.

"If you're finding it more challenging than ever to juggle the demands of your job and the rest of your life, you're not alone," says Jen Uscher in a *WebMD* Feature. Uscher suggests "five ways to bring a little more balance to your daily routine:

Build downtime into your schedule. Take time for family and friends. *Drop activities that sap your time and energy.* Maybe a little less time browsing the web can get you out of the office a little earlier. *Rethink your errands.* Can you outsource any of these things? *Get moving.* Build in time for exercise. *Remember that a little relaxation goes a long way.*[133] Plan a holiday. Get stuff done so that you can go home. Enjoy nature. Exercise. Do some gardening or lawn work. Get involved in community or religious organizations. Volunteer. Read a book. Listen to music. How about cleaning out the garage?

Mindfulness
Are We Missing Out on the Moment?

What is mindfulness? *Psychology Today* puts it this way: "Mindfulness is a state of active open attention on the present. When you're mindful, you observe your thoughts and feelings from a distance, without judging them good or bad. Instead of letting your life pass you by, mindfulness means living in the moment and awakening to experience."[134] Too often, moments pass, and we miss out. Just too busy. Consider each moment a gift.

Daniel Goleman, in his classic book, *Emotional Intelligence: Why It Can Matter More Than IQ*, ponders why some people, despite their IQ, do well, and others don't. Some of the difference can be attributed to emotional intelligence. He observes, "The ability to control impulse is the base of will and character. By the same token, the root of altruism lies in empathy, the ability to read the emotions of others. Lacking a sense of another's needs or despair, there is no caring. And if there are two moral stances that our times call for, they are precisely these, self-restraint and compassion."[135] Of course, we need to keep in mind that some conditions impair or limit control over emotions and may call for various therapies.

> **"The slogan of the hour shifted from the cheery 'Have a nice day' to the testiness of 'Make my day.'"**
> *Daniel Goleman*[136]

How Important is Work-Life Balance…?

In an always-on world, driven by demands for our attention, tons of twitters, emails as far as the eye can see, and schedules that press us from all sides, we depend on adrenalin to help us stay ahead of the curve. Sleep can sometimes be scarce. We often spend our weekends catching up on work or wearing ourselves out running errands or trying to reclaim our personal lives. Rather than continue to burn the candle at both ends, the time has come to admit one of the limits of our lifestyles and technologies—they can actually work us into a frenzy or even work us to death.

Then, there is health and wellness. Personal, organizational, and community health and wellness are like a foundation that supports our ability to enjoy and function. Exercise; eat healthy; and take care of yourself.[137] Remember, on average, we're living longer, and the body and mentality we have today may have to serve us for a long time. So let's try to avoid burnout or being too much of a *couch potato* or a *mouse potato*.

We'll let you take it from here.

Implications for Education and Society—*Personal Meaning and Work-Life Balance*

Implications are endless because this trend is so deeply ingrained in our lives. Hands down, we need to pay greater attention to emotional health, emotional intelligence, and the vast reaches of the affective domain. Baseline, we should rally a commitment to preparing students, educators, and our communities to pursue greater work-life balance.

• **Considering how business, government, education, and other institutions can contribute to work-life balance.** Two challenges.

First, we need to understand that it's OK to do those things, to unwire long enough to unwind and refresh. Second, we need to know how. Some people have been so busy for so long that they either feel guilty or have no idea what to do when they are presented with leisure time.

• **Paying more attention to both physical and emotional health and well-being.** With limited life experience, students need skills to cope with situations that may seem overwhelming—a bad grade, the loss of a boyfriend or girlfriend, a move, being bullied, or an economic downturn that puts college funds at risk. A thoughtful array of essential life and leadership skills could help students find perspective and give them a framework for dealing with emotional trauma that might otherwise lead to self-destructive behavior.

• **Making way for more people of all ages who are driven to move into education, public service careers, or just volunteer.** Among the many beliefs and attitudes we need to develop is an in-grained appreciation for people who work or volunteer in the public service. Too often, people, including politicians, judge our success by the size of a bank account rather than on our contributions to society.

Conclusion
Dealing with the Trends
Creating a Future is the Essence of Leadership

> **"Courage is not the absence of fear—
> it's inspiring others to move beyond it."**
> *Nelson Mandela*

Bold Steps to a Brighter Future

We all know that just maintaining the status quo can take more hours than there are in a day or days in a year. Therein lies the challenge. The world is moving at warp speed into a Global Knowledge/Information Age, and we're often trying to do even more perfectly what it takes to function in an Industrial Age.

How can we get a handle on the future? How can we demonstrate our intellectual leadership and breakthrough thinking? How can we energize our education system and our community? How can we take those exciting steps toward creating a new agenda for a world that is resetting for a whole new era?

Futures Processes
Getting and Staying Connected

One of the most basic of futures processes, or futures tools, is identifying, monitoring, and considering the implications of trends—but we won't stop there. We'll take a brief look at several of those tools, ranging from trend and issue analysis to gap analysis, and explore the idea of convening Community Conversations and Futures Councils. As we get the journey under way, let's also not forget we can become trendsetters, and we can raise issues. We have a golden opportunity to engage people in these futures processes.

Trend Analysis. *Twenty-One Trends for the 21ˢᵗ Century* zeroes in on revealing and dealing with the hundreds of these forces sweeping across the landscape. Each of us should try to become a *trend spotter*. We need to pay attention to every field, not just our own. Then, we might identity possible implications of those trends for how we run an organization or industry, for economic growth and development in our community, or for what students might need to know and be able to do to be prepared for the future.

Issue Management. This process kicks off by engaging a group in identifying some of the dozens of issues facing an organization, industry, profession, government, or nation. Once we've done that, we consider the *probability* or *likelihood* (a percentage, 90-10, 50-50, etc.) that each one will become a major issue for us. Then, we consider whether the issues will be of *high, medium, or low impact*. If an issue turns out to be high probability and high impact, we'd better manage it before it ends up managing us. You'll find a *probability/impact matrix* in the full *Twenty-One Trends* book.

Gap Analysis. Among the most exhilarating of these futures processes is *gap analysis*. Like trend and issue analysis, it gets people involved. In this case, have a diverse group envision characteristics or ideals for the organization we want or need to become. Then, ask them, on a scale of 1 to 10, to rate the institution on how well each statement currently describes how we're doing. Note the gap, and develop a plan of action to fill it. It's a process for paving the road in the direction you need or want to go.

Thinking across Trends. We've made clear in *Twenty-One Trends* that new ideas are often hatched in the white spaces or connective tissue between and among trends. We might ask, for example, "What are the implications of *aging* for *technology*…or implications of the *international/global* trend for *jobs and careers*?" That's prime ground for knowledge creation and breakthrough thinking.

Scenarios. Based on a variety of assumptions we might make, we can compose a series of three or four scenarios describing *alternative futures*. Scenarios have been described as "a coherent picture of a plausible future."[138]

My companion book, *Future-Focused Leadership: Preparing Schools, Students, and Communities for Tomorrow's Realities*, published by ASCD, focuses on these processes and provides greater detail on how they work.[139]

Engagement and Collaboration

How can we connect people? How can we bring them together in common purpose? We simply need to *engage people and let their ideas inform our decisions*. Not everyone will get what they want every time, but they'll know their voices have been heard and their ideas considered.

The possibilities? *Community Conversations* involve diverse groups of people in the processes we've just explained. *Futures Councils* and other *advisory bodies* can be an ongoing ear to the ground for us as we ask staff and community to share what they believe might be emerging issues or trends and to think with us about the implications of those forces we've addressed in *Twenty-One Trends*. We can expand the process with *crowdsourcing, systematic or informal surveys*, and *interviews*. We can reserve *agenda time* at internal and external meetings. Key words for leadership are *connected, collaborative*, and *inclusive*.

Putting the future squarely and constantly on the agenda is invigorating. It encourages *generative thinking*. Rather than complaining that "we don't have time to think," let's make *thinking* a part of our everyday business and engage a network of groups in the process. The discussion moves from excuses for yesterday to the excitement of creating a future. Everyone is enriched by a free, open, and ongoing discussion of trends.

Starting with the big picture and moving toward specifics generally makes more sense than trying to build a future on steamy arguments about current issues that suck all the air out of the room and leave little or no time for consideration of the future. If we want everyone in the same boat—all hands on deck—we need to let them on board.

Addressing the *Twenty-One Trends...* Some Suggestions

As you know, this booklet is a *Guide*, a condensation of the full book, *Twenty-One Trends for the 21st Century...Out of the Trenches and into the Future*, published by Education Week Press. That book presents in-depth information about each of the trends and detailed suggestions about how we can use them to stay in touch or put them to work in stimulating thinking about the future. The process can also breathe new life, energy, and enthusiasm into the organization. Here are a few steps you might want to consider:

• **First, obtain copies of** *Twenty-One Trends,* **a publication that is the basis for this** *Guide.* Provide them for as many people as possible, including those in a variety of leadership positions. Consider using the *Guide* as a handout to stimulate thinking far and wide about forces affecting our institutions. In an education system, that might include educators, parents, students, leaders in business and government, and others in the community.

• **Second, host a community conversation.** Consider participants for a system-wide Community Conversation. This diverse group might be comprised of people from a span of interests and backgrounds—and representative of the community. Of course, a number of staff and board members and possibly members of the media might also be engaged.

• **Third, develop an agenda and bring people together.** Share background materials, such as demographic information and these *Guides,* in advance or as part of the meeting. Feature a presentation on trends and issues. Include small-group (table group) brainstorming sessions (six to eight people to a group) focused on identifying possible *implications of trends.* Using a similar format, identify *issues* and sort them according to their probability and potential impact. Then, have participants do *gap analysis.* Each group should brainstorm from six to eight full-sentence descriptions (characteristics or ideals) of the organization we need to become. For the education system, each statement would describe, in broad terms, the system we need to get students ready for life in a fast-changing world. Together, rate each of the statements on a scale of 1 to 10, based on how well it represents current reality. Note the gaps, and consider what might be included in a plan of action to get from here to there. No problem if an item gets only 1, since we may have just hatched the idea. Ask for reasonably brief reports to the full group following each of these activities.

• **Fourth, collect and share information and ideas that have been generated.** Compile information and ideas that have been generated and share it as broadly as you think is appropriate. In some cases, you might want to do follow-up surveys or devote an agenda item or task force to some of the possibilities.

• **Fifth, consider ideas in planning, decision making, and in daily operations.** Learn from the thinking that has been shared; thank everyone for their wisdom; and offer periodic reports on how the ideas have enriched what we do. Again, make clear at all times that discussions and ideas generated by these groups are advisory. No votes. No consensus. Just ideas. The ideas will, however, help us make even better decisions and build a sense of ownership. *Keep the information in front of you as you consider or recommend programs, policies, and directions.*

• **Sixth, convene a network of Futures Councils.** Give thought to developing a network of Futures Councils. These diverse groups, made up of both staff and community, likely with rotating memberships, might meet a few times a year to engage as many people as possible. Their purpose is not to grind axes or lobby for special interests but to thoughtfully identify and share, possibly even study, trends and issues with implications for the institution. The thinking of these groups can be a significant resource as policies are considered and programs developed. These network provide a good way for boards and educators; business, government, and community leaders; and others to stay in touch and even better create a future in a fast-changing world.

> **"Insanity is doing the same thing over and over again and expecting different results."**
> *Albert Einstein*

Developing a Plan, Living Strategy, Strategic Vision
Make Planning a Continuous Process

Linear planning. It's been around for years, likely because it perpetuates itself. Planning is always hard work. However, it's easier when we put most of our energy into just moving the same things up, down, or sideways. How does anything new ever get on the agenda or into the plan? Linear plans might even be dangerous to our success or survival in what is fast becoming a non-linear world.

Flexibility, nimbleness, and vision should be built into our plan. That way, we can turn on a dime to pursue an opportunity or deal with a concern in a 24-7 world that just won't wait. To some extent, *we've lost the between* as we move from here to there. That makes most of us uncomfortable, but it's a reality we face. Bottom line: We need to turn our *strategic plans* into *strategic visions* and *living and evolving strategies* that can guide us as we build for a new tomorrow.

Trends can help us get an ongoing glimpse of what's just over the horizon or simply headed our way. We need to be true to our values and our heritage, but also nimble enough to quickly adjust our plan. Freeze the plan and the world will surge past us, leaving us as an island, disconnected from those we are pledged to serve. If that sounds disconcerting, it isn't. It's just a new way of thinking, a fresh mentality. In fact, our mentality shifts to becoming even better tomorrow, no matter how good we are today.

While we surely need to tackle today, we simply can't take our eye off tomorrow. We have an opportunity to build an even better world; create what truly are leadership organizations; demonstrate our ability to engage in knowledge creation and breakthrough thinking; and, perhaps selfishly, build our own legacies. It's time to get the process under way and keep it going.

Enjoy the journey as you constantly create an even better future.

Acknowledgments

My profound gratitude to members of the international *Futures Council 21*. This talented and intellectually generous council of 26 people from many parts of the nation and world responded to Delphi questionnaires, helping me identify, sort, and expand on issues and trends. For easy reference, Council members are listed at the end of this book.

I have been truly blessed to work with the seasoned and imaginative professionals who make my publisher, *Education Week* Press, a division of Editorial Projects in Education (EPE), one of the most respected and far-reaching in its field. I am particularly grateful to Publisher Michele Givens for her dedication to making my trends publications a part of the *Ed Week* family; Vice President for Research & Development Christopher Swanson, whose belief in this project made it possible; Director of Knowledge Services Rachael Delgado, who served as home-base for the project and provided ongoing support, counsel, and encouragement; and Program Associate Tim Ebner. My thanks also to Jaini Giannovario, who edited and helped shape the manuscript for publication; Director of Production Jo Arnone, Creative Director Laura Baker for her cover design, and Linda Jurkowitz for specifically designing the cover for this *Guide* and to all members of the EPE staff for their ongoing contributions to the cause. That, of course, includes EPE President and Editor Virginia Edwards, a longtime and treasured colleague.

Twenty-One Trends is the third book in this series. My thanks to staff members of the former Educational Research Service (ERS) for publishing the first two. I'm also grateful for information, ideas, and experiences generated by educators and others in many walks of life across the nation and world. Special thanks to colleagues associated with the World Future Society, the Center for Civic Education, and the Department of Defense Education Activity (DoDEA).

If you are among my mentors or those who have come to my presentations, studied my books, and considered or used my ideas, my deepest thanks. To all I've mentioned and multitudes of others anywhere in the world: Your wisdom continues to guide me.

I am especially grateful to my family. They have long supported my quest to seek, develop, explain, and encourage the thoughtful consideration of ideas for creating a more promising future.

Gary Marx

> **Note: If you can't connect...**Web sites listed as references are likely to change. If you search and draw a blank, first try your favorite search engine, such as Google, Yahoo, or Bing, to find the piece using the title of the work and perhaps the author. In some cases, items may have simply been removed from circulation.

References

1. Martin, Antoinette, "Defining the Buyer of the Future," *New York Times*, Feb. 6, 2009. http://www.nytimes.com/2009/02/08/realestate/08njzo.html.

2. Chase, Howard, *Issue Management: Origin of the Future*. Issue Action Publications, Stamford, CT, 1984, p. 38.

3. *Webster's New Collegiate Dictionary*. Merriam-Webster Inc., Springfield, MA, 2003, p. 1,334.

4. Barry, Dan, "Boomers Hit New Self-Absorption Milestone: Age 65," *New York Times*, Dec. 31, 2010. http://www.nytimes.com/2011/01/01/us/01boomers.html?_r=1.

5. "Turning 30," a series of articles about Millennials turning 30 years of age, *Huffington Post*. http://www.huffingtonpost.com/news/turning-30.

6. Strauss, William, and Howe, Neil, "Cycles in U.S. History, Remembering the Future," based on research by generational experts, such as, *The Time Page*. http://www.timepage.org/time.html#cycles.

7. Strauss, William, and Howe, Neil, "Global Generations and Global Aging: A Fifty-Year Outlook," presentation at World Future Society 9th General Assembly, Washington, DC, 1999.

8. Strauss, William, and Howe, Neil, *The Fourth Turning...An American Prophesy*, Broadway Books, a division of Bantam Doubleday Dell Publishing Group, Inc., NY, 1998, p. 3.

9. "GI Generation (Born 1912-1927)," The Intergenerational Center, Temple University. http://cil.templecil.org/node/35.

10. Honisch, Marty; Leaf, Margaret; and Ryan, Rebecca, "Where are the Next Cities?" Area Development Online, (drawing from observations of Richard Florida). http://www.areadevelopment.com/siteSelection/august09/next-generation-cities-knowledge-workers.shtml.

11. Friese, Lauren, and Jowett, Cassandra, of TalentEgg, "The Six Ways Generation Y Will Transform the Workplace," *Globe and Mail,* Canada, March 12, 2013. http://www.theglobeandmail.com/report-on-business/careers/the-future-of-work/the-six-ways-generation-y-will-transform-the-workplace/article9615027/

12. Gandhi, Mahatma, Brainy Quote. http://www.brainyquote.com/quotes/quotes/m/mahatmagan160841.html.

13. Yen, Hope, "White Population to Lose Majority Status in 2043," *Associated Press, The Boston Globe,* Dec. 13, 2012. http://www.bostonglobe.com/news/nation/2012/12/13/census-whites-longer-majority/cldoCAQfjIWT34hnhmXFAM/story.html.

14. Frey, William H., "Census Projects New "Majority Minority" Tipping Points, Brookings Institution, Opinion, State of Metropolitan America, No. 58 of 61, data used in two illustrations, "Year When Non-Hispanic White Become a Minority, By Age Group" and "Projected U.S. General Population by

Race/Ethnicity, 2012 and 2060: Total Population, Youth Under 18, Seniors 65+, Percentages." http://www.brookings.edu/research/opinions/2012/12/13-census-race-projections-frey.

15. "U.S. Whites Now Losing Majority in Under-5 Age Group as Deaths Outnumber Births for First Time," *Washington Post Business,* Associated Press, June 13, 2013. http://www.washingtonpost.com/local/white-deaths-outnumber-births-for-first-time/2013/06/13/3bb1017c-d388-11e2-a73e-826d299ff459_story.html.

16. U.S. Census Bureau, International Data Base, Comparing 2000 and 2050. http://www.census.gov/population/international/data/idb/informationGateway.php.

17. Bernstein, Robert, "Most Children Younger than Age 1 are Minorities," *Census Bureau Reports,* U.S. Census Bureau News Release, May 17 2012. http://www.census.gov/newsroom/releases/archives/population/cb12-90.html.

18. Chevalier, Maurice quotes, Brainy Quotes. http://www.brainyquote.com/quotes/authors/m/maurice_chevalier.html.

19. Marx, Gary. This item is based on multiple references included in Tables T2.1, T3.1, T3.2, and T3.3, included in the full version of *Twenty-One Trends for the 21st Century,* 2014, featuring information from the U.S. Census Bureau, pp. 52, 82, 84, 86.

20. U.S. Census Data, *Info Please,* Pearson Education, Inc., "Life Expectancy at Birth by Race and Sex, 1930-2010," Both Sexes, and "Life Expectancy by Age, 1850-2004," sexes listed separately, 2011. http://www.infoplease.com/ipa/A0005148.html. Compared with "Life Expectancy in the USA, 1900-98, Men and Women." http://demog.berkeley.edu/~andrew/1918/figure2.html, and Sullivan, Patricia, Washington Post, "U.S. Life Expectancy Rises, But Bad Habits Persist," July 11, 2013, p. A-6.

21. Wallace, Paul, *Agequake: Riding the Demographic Rollercoaster Shaking Business, Finance, and Our World,* Nicholas Brealey Publishing, Ltd., London, 1999, p. 5-6.

22. U.S. Census Bureau, "Population Projections, 2000 National Population Projections, Summary Tables." http://www.census.gov/population/projections/data/national/natsum.html, click on appropriate individual tables.

23. *The New York Times Almanac,* "Births and Deaths in the U.S., 1910-2008." Birth Rate, per thousand reduced to per hundred by author, 2011, New York Times Company, NY, p.294.

24. U.S. Census Bureau, "Live Births, Deaths, Marriages, and Divorces: 1960 to 2007, Table 78, Statistical Abstract of the U.S., 2011." http://www.census.gov/compendia/statab/2011/tables/11s0078.pdf.

25. "Fertility Rates, Michigan and U.S. Residents, Selected Years, 1900-2011." http://www.mdch.state.mi.us/pha/osr/natality/tab1.3.asp; and *National Vital Statistics Reports,* Vol. 61, No. 1, Aug. 28, 2012. http://www.cdc.gov/nchs/data/nvsr/nvsr61/nvsr61_01.pdf.

26. Centers for Diseases Control and Prevention (CDC), "Deaths and Mortality." http://www.cdc.gov/nchs/fastats/deaths.htm.

27. National Center for Health Statistics 2000, Table 1. In Marx, Gary, *Ten Trends,* Educational Research Service, Arlington, VA, 2000. p. 6.

28. U.S. Census Bureau, International Data Base, Demographic Overview, Crude Death Rate per 1,000 Population. http://www.census.gov/population/international/data/idb/informationGateway.php, Feb. 28, 2012.

29. "2011 Technical Panel on Assumptions and Methods, Report to the Social Security Advisory Board," Sept. 2011. http://www.ssab.gov/Reports/2011_TPAM_Final_Report.pdf. "Ratio of Covered Workers to Beneficiaries." http://www.ssa.gov/history/ratios.html. "Life Expectancy at Birth by Race and Sex, 1930 to 2010." http://www.infoplease.com/ipa/A0005148.html. and "Life Expectancy for Social Securi-

ty," Social Security Administration. http://www.ssa.gov/history/lifeexpect.html.

30. U.S. Census Bureau, International Data Base, "Total Mid-Year Population of the World, 1950-2050." http://www.census.gov/population/international/data/idb/worldpoptotal.php. U.S. Census Bureau, "Total Midyear Population for the World: 1950-2050," U.S. Pop Clock, Worldometer. http://www.census.gov/population/www/popclockus.html.

31. U.S. Department of Education, National Center for Education Statistics (2012). *Digest of Education Statistics, 2011* (NCES 2012-001), Chapter 1, "Fast Facts, Enrollment Trends." http://nces.ed.gov/fastfacts/display.asp?id=65.

32. U.S. Department of Education, "Projections of Education Statistics to 2020," National Center for Education Statistics, "Actual and Projected Numbers for Enrollment in All Postsecondary Degree-Granting Institutions: Fall 1995 through fall 2020." http://nces.ed.gov/programs/projections/projections2020/tables/table_22.asp?referrer=list.

33. Brownstein, Joseph, "Most Babies Born Today May Live Past 100," ABC News Medical Unit, *ABC News,* Oct. 1, 2009. http://abcnews.go.com/Health/WellnessNews/half-todays-babies-expected-live-past-100/story?id=8724273.

34. U.S. Census Bureau, "Older Americans Month: May 2012," Profile America Facts for Features, March 1, 2012. http://www.census.gov/newsroom/releases/archives/facts_for_features_special_editions/cb12-ff07.html.

35. Markoff, John, "Computer Wins on 'Jeopardy!': Trivial, It's Not," *New York Times,* Feb. 16, 2011. http://www.nytimes.com/2011/02/17/science/17jeopardy-watson.html.

36. Lohr, Steve, "The Age of Big Data," *New York Times,* Feb. 11, 2012. http://www.nytimes.com/2012/02/12/sunday-review/big-datas-impact-in-the-world.html.

37. Strickland, Jonathan, "How Cloud Computing Works," *How Stuff Works,* A Discovery Company. http://computer.howstuffworks.com/cloud-computing/cloud-computing.htm.

38. University of Oxford, Oxford Martin School, News, "The Next Technological Revolutions," report on presentation by Eric Drexler of the Foresight Institute. http://www.oxfordmartin.ox.ac.uk/news/201111-news-FutureTechLaunch.

39. Ford, Dale, "Intel's Semiconductor Market Share Surges to More Than 10-Year High in 2011," HIS Supply Market Research, March 26, 2012.

40. Peckham, Matt, "The Collapse of Moore's Law: Physicist Says It's Already Happening," *Time Techland, Innovation,* May 1, 2012. http://techland.time.com/2012/05/01/the-collapse-of-moores-law-physicist-says-its-already-happening/.

41. Burton, Jeff; Kinter, Marcia; and Marx, Dan, 2005 *Guide to Digital Imaging,* 2004, Specialty Graphic Imaging Association/Digital Printing and Imaging Association, Fairfax, VA, 2004, pp. 1, 7-9.

42. "Using 21st Century Tools for College Success, This Week's Top Educator Resource," promotion announcement, *eSchool News Online.*

43. Dede, Chris, Presentation and Comments during Harvard Future of Learning Institute, Cambridge, Mass., Aug. 2, 2012.

44. World Bank, Information and Communication Technologies, "Maximizing Mobile Report Highlights Development Potential of Mobile Communications," July 17, 2012. http://web.worldbank.org/WBSITE/EXTERNAL/COUNTRIES/MENAEXT/GTOPPOVRED/0,,contentMDK:23242711-menuPK:497128~pagePK:2865114~piPK:2865167~theSitePK:497110,00.html.

45. Heller, Joseph, quotes. http://www.goodreads.com/author/quotes/3167.Joseph_Heller.

46. Turkle, Sherry, "Connected, but alone?" *TED Talk*, Sherry Turkle, posted April 2012. http://www. ted.com/talks/sherry_turkle_alone_together.html.

47. Richtel, Matt, "Silicon Valley Says Step Away From the Device," *New York Times*, July 23, 2012. http://www.nytimes.com/2012/07/24/technology/silicon-valley-worries-about-addiction-to-devices. html.

48. U.S. Department of Education, "Family Educational Rights and Privacy Act (FERPA)." http:// www2.ed.gov/policy/gen/guid/fpco/ferpa/index.html.

49. "What is FOIA?". http://www.foia.gov.

50. "Spotlight on Social Media in the Classroom," *Education Week*. http://www.edweek.org/ew/market-place/products/spotlight-social-media-in-the-classroom.html.

51. Federal Trade Commission, "About Identity Theft: Deter, Detect, Defend, and Avoid ID Theft." http://www.in.gov/isp/files/IDT01-ddd.pdf.

52. Gunther, Marc, "Immelt: We Are in an Emotional, Social, Economic Reset," *GreenBiz.com*, Nov. 8, 2008. http://www.greenbiz.com/blog/2008/11/08/immelt-we-are-emotional-social-economic-reset.

53. American Society of Civil Engineers (ASCE), "Report Card for American Infrastructure." http:// www.infrastructurereportcard.org/.

54. Frey, Thomas, "2011 in Review, 55 Jobs of the Future." http://www.futuristspeaker.com/2011/11/55-jobs-of-the-future/.

55. U.S. Bureau of Labor Statistics (BLS), "Usual Weekly Earnings of Wage and Salary Workers, Third Quarter, 2012," Table 5. http://www.bls.gov/news.release/pdf/wkyeng.pdf.

56. Florida, Richard, "Creatives and the Crisis," *The Atlantic*, Oct. 22, 2012. http://www.citylab.com/work/2012/10/creatives-and-crisis/1727/.

57. Florida, Richard, *The Great Reset*, Harper-Collins, NY, 2010/2011, pp 116-128.

58. Gallman, Robert E., "Trends in the Location of Population, Industry, and Employment, Ohio State University, Table 1. http://ageconsearch.umn.edu/bitstream/17629/1/ar610017.pdf, based on information from Historical Statistics of the United States, Bureau of the Census, 1960, p 74.

59. U.S. Bureau of Labor Statistics, "Employment Projections. Employment by Major Industry Sector," Table 2.1. http://data.bls.gov/cgi-bin/print.pl/emp/ep_table_201.htm.

60. U.S. Department of Labor, Bureau of Labor Statistics, "Fastest Growing Occupations, 2002-2012" and "Occupations with the Largest Job Declines, 2002-2012," *Monthly Labor Review*, February 2004. http://www.bls.gov/news.release/archives/ecopro_02112004.pdf.

61. U.S Bureau of Labor Statistics, "Projections Overview," Table 1, Occupations with the Fastest Growth, Projected 2010-2020,"and "Table 3, Occupations with the Fastest Decline, Projected 2010-2020." http:// www.bls.gov/opub/mlr/2012/01/art5full.pdf.

62. Bascuas, Katie, "So You've Decided to Implement Teleworking. Now What?" *Associations Now*, May 2, 2013. http://associationsnow.com/2013/05/so-youve-decided-to-implement-teleworking-now-what/.

63. Wagner, Cynthia G., "Emerging Careers and How to Create Them," *The Futurist*, Jan.-Feb. 2011, p 30.

64. "Employability Skills: SCANS Profile." http://www.learningconnections.org/ss/pdfs/biotechnology-biomedical/bio4.pdf.

65. Caprino, Kathy, "What You Don't Know Will Hurt You: The Top 8 Skills Professionals Need to Master," *Forbes*, April 27, 2012. http://www.forbes.com/sites/kathycaprino/2012/04/27/what-you-dont-know-will-hurt-you-the-top-8-skills-professionals-need-to-master/.

66. The Conference Board of Canada, "Employability Skills 2000+." http://www.conferenceboard.ca/topics/education/learning-tools/employability-skills.

67. Gordon, Edward, presentation, World Future Society Annual Conference, Chicago, Ill., July 20, 2013. Gordon is author of *Future Jobs: Solving the Employment and Skills Crisis*, Praeger, Chicago, Sept. 2013.

68. Pennsylvania Department of Education, "Career Education & Work (CEW) Standards Toolkit." http://www.pacareerstandards.com/.

69. *Worldchanging: A User's Guide for the 21st Century*, edited by Steffen, Alex; introduction by McKibben, Bill, Abrams, NY, 2011. http://www.amazon.com/Worldchanging-Users-Guide-21st-Century/dp/0810970856.

70. U.S. Department of Energy, "Understanding Earth's Energy Sources," Energy Education and Workforce Development. http://www1.eere.energy.gov/education/pdfs/acts_harrell_understandingfossilfuels_307.pdf.

71. U.S. Energy Information Administration, "U.S. Energy Facts, Explained, Consumption & Production, Americans Use Many Type of Energy." http://www.eia.gov/energyexplained/print.cfm?page=us_energy_home, updated Oct. 15, 2012.

72. Advanced Power & Energy, University of California at Irvine, "Building Templates: Commercial Buildings: Education Buildings," 2007.

73. "USA's 20th Century Power Grid Fails Its 21st Century Economy," *USA Today*, Opinion, Our View, Nov. 13, 2012, p. 8a.

74. Electrochemical Society, "Large Scale Energy Storage for Smart Grid Applications," *ecstransactions*, Vol. 41, No. 23. http://ecst.ecsdl.org/content/41/23/local/front-matter.pdf.

75. U.S. Department of Energy, "Energy Literacy…Essential Principles and Fundamental Concepts for Energy Education, A framework for Energy Education for Learners of All Ages." http://www1.eere.energy.gov/education/pdfs/energy_literacy_1_0_low_res.pdf.

76. Goodall, Jane, interviewed on *Bill Moyers Journal, PBS*, Nov. 27, 2009. http://www.pbs.org/moyers/journal/11272009/watch.html.

77. Gillis, Justin, "Heat-Trapping Gas Passes Milestone, Raises Fears," *New York Times*, May 10, 2013. http://www.nytimes.com/2013/05/11/science/earth/carbon-dioxide-level-passes-long-feared-milestone.html?.

78. "About Six Degrees Could Change the World," *National Geographic* television program. http://natgeotv.com/ca/six_degrees/about.

79. Rifkin, Jeremy, *The Third Industrial Revolution*, Palgrave Macmillan, NY, 2012, p 13.

80. Thoreau, Henry, quote, *Great Quotes.com*. www.great-quotes.com/quote/759537.

81. "Sustainable," definition, synonyms and antonyms, *Merriam-Webster Online Dictionary*. http://www.merriam-webster.com/dictionary/sustainable.

82. Fiksel, Joseph; Eason, Tasha; and Frederickson, Herbert, "A Framework for Sustainability, Indicators at EPA," National Risk Management Research Laboratory, Office of Research and Development, U.S. Environmental Protection Agency (EPA), Oct. 2012. http://cfpub.epa.gov/si/si_public_record_Report.cfm?dirEntryID=254270.

83. Engelman, Robert, *Vital Signs*, 2011, The Worldwatch Institute, Washington, DC. In section devoted to "World Population Growth Slows Modestly, Still on Track for 7 Billion in Late 2011," Table 1, Regional Population Basics for 2010, Share of Absolute Global Population. Data from U.N. Population Division. http://esa.un.org/unup/.

84. Friedman, Thomas L., *The World is Flat…A Brief History of the 21st Century,* 2005-2006-2007, Farrar, Straus and Giroux, NY.

85. Harvard Graduate School of Education, "Future of Learning: Strand 3: Globalization" introductory materials, Future of Learning Institute, Aug. 3, 2012.

86. U.S. Census Bureau, International Data Base, "World Population: 1950-2050." http://www.census.gov/population/international/data/idb/worldpopgraph.php.

87. Gardner, Lauren, "Worldwide Urbanization," *World Politics Review,* June 28, 2007. http://www.worldpoliticsreview.com/trend-lines/895/worldwide-urbanization.

88. Reimers, Fernando M., "Leading for Global Competency," *Educational Leadership,* Sept. 2009, Volume 67, Number 1. http://www.ascd.org/publications/educational-leadership/sept09/vol67/num01/Leading-for-Global-Competency.aspx.

89. "Methodology-Teaching Diplomacy," Diplo Foundation, Malta and Geneva, 1999-2005, originally accessed in 2005. Diplomacy Foundation web site is at http://www.diplomacy.edu/. Original information appeared in the *Sixteen Trends* book by Gary Marx, pp. 251-252, but no longer online, retrieved on March 7, 2005, from http://www.diplomacy.edu/Edu/Methodology/teaching.asp.

90. "Putting the World into World-Class Education, State Innovations and Opportunities," CCSSO and the Asia Society. http://asiasociety.org/files/stateinnovations.pdf.

91. *Edudemic,* "30 Dr. Seuss Quotes You Should Never Forget." http://www.edudemic.com/30-dr-seuss-quotes-you-should-never-forget/.

92. Personalized Learning. http://en.wikipedia.org/wiki/Personalized_learning.

93. U.S Department of Education, "Individualized, Personalized, and Differentiated Instruction." http://www.ed.gov/technology/draft-netp-2010/individualized-personalized-differentiated-instruction.

94. Common Core Standards, "Frequently Asked Questions." http://www.corestandards.org/about-the-standards/frequently-asked-questions/.

95. Hymes, Donald, with Chafin, Ann, and Gonder, Peggy, *The Changing Face of Testing and Assessment,* American Association of School Administrators, 1991, p. 4.

96. Immordino-Yang, M.H. and Fischer, K.W., "Neuroscience Bases of Learning," Elsevier, Ltd., 2012, page 310, reading for 2012 Harvard University Future of Learning Institute. Immordino-Yang, M.H., & Fischer, K.W. (2009, in press). Neuroscience bases of learning. In V.G. Aukrust (Ed.), *International Encyclopedia of Education,* 3rd Edition, Section on Learning and Cognition, Oxford, England: Elsevier. http://www-bcf.usc.edu/~immordin/papers/Immordino-Yang+Fischer_2009_NeuroscienceBasesofLearning.pdf.

97. Gardner, Howard, *Multiple Intelligences, The Theory in Practice,* BasicBooks, a division of HarperCollins Publishers, Inc., 1993, drawn from pp. 15-27.

98. Item based on stories/news releases from SIIA and ASCD, including: "District Race to the Top Appropriately Prioritizes Personalized Learning." http://www.siia.net/blog/index.php/2012/05/district-race-to-the-top-appropriately-prioritizes-personalized-learning/, and "Education Leaders Identify Top 10 Components of Personalized Learning." http://www.ascd.org/news-media/Press-Room/News-Releases/Education-Leaders-Identify-Top-10-Components-of-Personalized-Learning.aspx.

99. Denvir, Daniel, "School: It's Way More Boring Than When You Were There," Salon.com, Sept. 14, 2011. http://www.salon.com/2011/09/14/denvir_school/.

100. Perkins, David, Presentation during Harvard University Future of Learning Institute, Cambridge, MA, July 31, 2012.

101. Einstein, Albert, quotes, Quote from interview with G.S. Viereck, Oct. 26, 1929. Reprinted in

"Glimpses of the Great" (1930). http://einstein.biz/quotes.php.

102. Robinson, Kenneth, *TED Talk,* http://www.ted.com/speakers/sir_ken_robinson.

103. Sparks, Sarah D., "Studies Explore How to Nurture Students' Creativity," *Education Week,* Dec. 13, 2011. http://www.edweek.org/ew/articles/2011/12/14/14creative.h31.html.

104. Ibid., 100

105. Perkins, David, and Tishman, Shari, "Patterns of Thinking," Project Zero, Harvard University. http://www.pz.gse.harvard.edu/patterns_of_thinking.php.

106. Costa, Arthur L., "The Thought-Filled Curriculum," *Educational Leadership,* ASCD, Feb.2008, pp. 20-24. http://www.ascd.org/publications/educational_leadership/feb08/vol65/num05/The_Thought-Filled_Curriculum.aspx.

107. Ibid., 96.

108. Gardner, Howard, *Five Minds for the Future,* Harvard Business School Press, Cambridge, MA, 2007.

109. Perkins, David, Presentation during Harvard University Future of Learning Institute, Cambridge, MA, July 31, 2012.

110. Hirsch, Jr., E.D.; Kett, Joseph F.; and Trefil, James, *The Dictionary of Cultural Literacy...What Every American Needs to Know,* Houghton Mifflin Company, Boston, 1988, p. 300.

111. Friedman, Thomas L., "Advice from Grandma," *New York Times,* Nov. 22, 2009. http://www.ny-times.com/2009/11/22/opinion/22friedman.html.

112. "Definitions of Authority, Authoritarian," *Merriam-Webster Dictionary Online.* http://www.merriam-webster.com/dictionary/authority, http://www.merriam-webster.com/dictionary/authoritative, http://www.merriam-webster.com/dictionary/authoritarian.

113. *Webster's New Collegiate Dictionary,* Merriam-Webster, Inc., NY, 1983, p. 426.

114. State Secretariat for Economic Affairs (SECO), "What is Corruption?" http://www.seco.admin.ch/themen/00645/00657/00659/01387/.

115. Kidder, Rushworth, quote from Rushworth Kidder, founder of the Institute for Global Ethics, from his book, Moral Courage, William Morrow Paperbacks, NY, 2009, p. 3.

116. Hausman, Carl, Editor, "The Top 10 Ethics Stories of 2012". http://carlhausman.com/2013/01/21/the-top-10-ethics-stories-of-2012/.

117. Murrow, Edward R. quote, *ASCD Smart Brief,* Feb. 8, 2012.

118. Character Counts, Los Angeles, California, "Six Pillars of Character." http://charactercounts.org/sixpillars.html.

119. Josephson, Michael, president of Character Counts, quotes. http://www.goodreads.com/author/quotes/1090178.Michael_Josephson.

120. Tang, Mei-Ying, "Human Rights Education in Taiwan: The Experience of the Workshops for Schoolteachers." http://www.hurights.or.jp/archives/human_rights_education_in_asian_schools/section2/1999/03/human-rights-education-in-taiwan-the-experience-of-the-workshops-for-schoolteachers.html.

121. Franklin, Benjamin, "Ben Franklin's Two Daily Questions and 13 Virtues," Ethics Alarms. http://ethicsalarms.com/rule-book/ben-franklins-two-daily-questions-and-13-virtues/.

122. Deming, W. Edwards, *Out of the Crisis,* Massachusetts Institute of Technology, Center for Advanced Engineering Study, Cambridge, Massachusetts, 1991, pp. 23-24.

123. Holiday, Billie, and Herzog, Arthur Jr., "God Bless The Child," Lyrics to song, written by Billie Holiday and Arthur Herzog, Jr., Carlin America, Inc., Warner/Chappell Music, Inc. EMI Music Publishing. http://www.lyricsfreak.com/b/billie+holiday/god+bless+the+child_20018000.html.

124. National Center for Children in Poverty (NCCP). "Child Poverty." http://www.nccp.org/topics/childpoverty.html.

125. The World Bank, "Poverty Reduction and Equity, At a Glance." http://www.worldbank.org/en/topic/poverty/overview

126. Rebell, Michael A. and Wolff, Jessica R., "We Can Overcome Poverty's Impact on School Success," *Education Week* Commentary, Jan. 18, 2012. http://www.edweek.org/ew/articles/2012/01/18/17rebell.h31.html.

127. World Bank, "Share of World's Private Consumption, 2005," Poverty Facts and Stats, Global Issues. http://www.globalissues.org/article/26/poverty-facts-and-stats, updated Jan. 7, 2013.

128. Wright Edelman, Marian, President, Children's Defense Fund, "Families Struggle: Child Poverty Remains Epidemically High," *Huffington Post*, Sept. 28, 2012. http://www.huffingtonpost.com/marian-wright-edelman/families-struggle-child-p_b_1924179.html.

129. Rifkin, Jeremy, *The Third Industrial Revolution, How Lateral Power is Transforming Energy, The Economy, and The World*, Palgrave Macmillan, NY, 2011, p. 238.

130. Domhoff, G. William, "Wealth, Income, and Power," WhoRulesAmerica.net, 2013. http://www2.ucsc.edu/whorulesamerica/power/wealth.html.

131. Elert, Emily, Writer; De Chant, Tim, Illustrator, "Daily Infographic: If Everyone Lived Like An American, How Many Earths Would We Need?" http://www.popsci.com/environment/article/2012-10/daily-infographic-if-everyone-lived-american-how-many-earths-would-we-need?.

132. Creagan, Edward T., "Stress Management, Don't Forget the 'Life' in Work-Life Balance," Stress Blog, *MayoClinic.com*, Feb. 19, 2010. http://www.mayoclinic.com/health/work-life-balance/MY01203.

133. Uscher, Jen, "Beat Burnout by Making More Time for the Activities and People That Matter Most to You," *WebMD* Feature. http://www.webmd.com/health-insurance/protect-health-13/balance-life, article also features quotes from psychologist Robert Brooks and productivity expert Laura Stack. The titles of their books are included in the corresponding section of *Twenty-One Trends*.

134. "Mindfulness," *Psychology Today* (online).http://www.psychologytoday.com/basics/mindfulness.

135. Goleman, Daniel, *Emotional Intelligence,* Bantam Books, NY, 2005, p. xxii.

136. Goleman, Daniel, *Emotional Intelligence,* Tenth Anniversary Edition, Book (1995), Introduction (2005), Bantam, NY, p. xxi.

137. National Institutes of Health, "Science-Based Health & Wellness Resources for Your Community." http://www.nih.gov/health/wellness/.

138. "Scenarios," RAND Europe. www.rand.org/randeurope/fields/scenarios.html, search "scenarios," 2013. Also Marx, Gary, *Future-Focused Leadership*, ASCD, Alexandria, VA, 2006, p. 119.

139. Marx, Gary, *Future-Focused Leadership: Preparing Schools, Students, and Communities for Tomorrow's Realities,* ASCD, 2005.

Futures Council 21

Beginning in the fall of 2012, members of an international Futures Council 21 agreed to provide ideas and thoughtful counsel for the author in shaping this book, which became *Twenty-One Trends for the 21st Century*. The 26 members of this distinguished advisory council responded to either one or two rounds of questionnaires in a modified Delphi process. As author, I know I speak for all readers, including countless people in education and many other walks of life, in many parts of the world, who will benefit from the thinking of this eloquent group of visionary leaders.

Views expressed in *Twenty-One Trends* do not necessarily reflect the beliefs or opinions of any member of Futures Council 21, the Council as a whole, or their organizations, nor do they reflect the official views of the publisher, Education Week Press, Editorial Projects in Education. The book is designed to be a marketplace of information and provocative ideas.

Members of Futures Council 21 included: **Stephen Aguilar-Millan**, director of research, The European Futures Observatory, Ipswich, U.K.; **Meera Balachandran**, director, Education Quality Foundation of India, Gurgaon, Haryana, India; **Laurie Barron**, 2013 MetLife/ NASSP National Middle Level Principal of the Year, who became superintendent of the Evergreen School District in Montana; **Sheldon Berman**, superintendent of the Eugene Public Schools in Eugene, Oregon; **Joseph J. Cirasuolo**, executive director, Connecticut Association of Public School Administrators, West Hartford, Connecticut; **Avis Glaze**, president of Edu-quest International, Inc., and former chief student achievement officer for Ontario, Canada. She is now in British Columbia; **Joseph Hairston**, president and CEO of Vision Unlimited, LLC, and immediate past superintendent of the Baltimore County Public Schools in Maryland; **James Harvey**, executive director, National Superintendents Roundtable, Seattle, Washington; **Debra Hill**, associate professor, Argosy University, Chicago, longtime school administrator and 2012 national ASCD president; **Ryan Hunter**, a student leader and future-focused scholar at The American University in Washington, D.C.; **Frank Kwan**, director of communications services for the Los Angeles County Office of Education in California; **Damian LaCroix**, superintendent, Howard-Suamico School District, Green Bay, Wisconsin; **Allison LaFave**, a recent Harvard graduate, serving as marketing, communication, and development associate for Legal Outreach in New York City; **Anash Mangalparsad**, director, Centre for Community and Educational Development, South Africa. He called upon Jessica Vinod Kumar, a teacher at M.L. Sultan (Pmb) Secondary School in Pietermaritzburg, South Africa, to respond to questions; **Keith Marty**, superintendent, Parkway School District, Chesterfield, Missouri; **John Meagher**, professional futurist, Manassas, Virginia; **Rebecca Mieliwocki**, 7th grade English teacher at Luther Burbank Middle School in Burbank, California, and 2012 National Teacher of the Year; **Matthew Moen**, dean of the College of Arts & Sciences at the University of South Dakota in Vermillion and a recent president of the national Council of Colleges of Arts & Sciences; **Stephen Murley**, superintendent, Iowa City Community School District, Iowa City, Iowa; **Patrick Newell**, learning activist and "vision navigator" of the Tokyo International School in Japan, also president of the 21 Foundation; **Marcus Newsome**, superintendent, Chesterfield County Public Schools, Chesterfield, Virginia; **Concepción Olavarrieta**, president, Nodo Mexicano, El Proyecto del Milenio, A.C. (Mexico's U.N. Millennium Project) Mexico City; **Gary Rowe**, media producer, communications consultant, and president, Rowe, Inc., Lawrenceville, Georgia; **David Pearce Snyder**, futurist and contributing editor, *The Futurist Magazine*, Bethesda, Maryland; **Michael Usdan**, senior fellow, Institute for Educational Leadership, Washington, D.C.; and **Milde Waterfall**, teacher, retired from Thomas Jefferson High School for Science and Technology, Fairfax County, Virginia.

About the Author

Gary Marx, CAE, APR, is a noted author, futurist, executive, consultant, and international speaker. As a futurist, Marx has directed a number of studies and written numerous books and articles. Just prior to *Twenty-One Trends for the 21st Century,* his best-selling books included *Sixteen Trends...Their Profound Impact on Our Future,* which highlighted key forces reshaping our world, and *Future-Focused Leadership,* a motivating guide for creating an even brighter future.

Marx is president of the Center for Public Outreach, in Vienna, Va. an organization he founded that provides counsel on future-oriented leadership, communication, education, community, and democracy. He has been called an "intellectual entrepreneur, who is constantly pursuing ideas" and a "deep generalist." During his career, he has worked with a broad range of educators, business people, and other community and government leaders.

His international speaking and consulting assignments have taken him to six continents. A few examples include the northern Andean region of Peru, desert areas of Jordan, the Pacific coast of Russia, communities across Senegal, the eastern coast of Australia, and many parts of Europe and Asia. Those assignments in North America include all 50 of the United States, most provinces of Canada, and many states of Mexico. He has visited more than 80 countries.

Marx, who acts both locally and globally, has been especially inspired by his work with students and educators who are developing civic education projects to improve life in their communities and countries. He is an on-the-ground communicator who attempts to understand people and issues and offer leadership and counsel on numerous fronts, from advising on the Bicentennial of the U.S. Constitution to working with his home communities to help create parks and monuments. Gary Marx has been recognized with the President's Award from the National School Public Relations Association and the Distinguished Service Award from the American Association of School Administrators. Marx and his wife, Judy, live in Vienna, Va. He can be reached at gmarxcpo@aol.com.